$1.50

P9-CJY-218

Kindergarten Minute by Minute

Timy Baranoff

Fearon Pitman Publishers, Inc.
Belmont, California

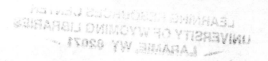

Edited by Rudite Emir
Designed by Faron Studios, Inc.
Cover design by Wayne and Linda Bonnett
Design management by Kauthar Hawkins

ISBN-0-8224-4100-4

Library of Congress Catalog Card Number: 78-72076

Printed in the United States of America.

1.9 8 7 6 5 4

Contents

V. Art, 49

VI. Music, 67

VII. Study Time, 79

VIII. Resource People, 95

IX. Room Management, 99

Epilogue, 107

Appendix, 109

Introduction

MANY excellent books delineate the history of the development of schools specifically designed for young children in the United States. Other books outline various kinds of programs in different parts of the country, or describe present-day concerns, innovative programs, or results of recent research related to early childhood education. This book is not intended to duplicate the efforts of any of these fine publications but is designed, rather, to offer some practical help to teachers by sharing information and ideas accrued from my dozen years of teaching young children, from my training of students interested in becoming teachers, and from my studies toward a Ph.D. in curriculum and instruction, with an emphasis on early childhood education.

New teachers often go through a very difficult period of time in the first few weeks or first year in their new role. Sadly, there is a high attrition rate after the first few months or first year of teaching. Some new teachers last only a few weeks. I have felt for some time that many of the anxieties experienced at the beginning of this new career could have been alleviated and serious problems solved or avoided if help of a more practical nature would have been made available. Piaget's theories on the development of the intellect are interesting indeed, and important to know, but hardly essential at that moment when fifteen to twenty-five children arrive at the door on the first day of school.

One of the most difficult tasks facing the new teacher is to plan for and execute a successful first day. A first day that succeeds is not a chance occurrence but takes place because of careful preparations the teacher has made in anticipation of the first day with the children.

First days are very important, for at this time the teacher begins to build a happy, working, student-teacher relationship—one that will be built on mutual trust. What occurs in the first days can also influence the parent-teacher relationship. And if ever a classroom is described as one without discipline problems, it would follow that it is a classroom where good management practices were set in motion on the very first day of school and reinforced every day thereafter. Teachers with a reputation for good management set the "tone" for the school year early. The successful teacher is also aware of the importance of quickly establishing routines for the children. All that is going to be included as part of every school day is included in the first day—only within a shorter time frame.

This book places a great deal of emphasis on the first days, for I feel that successful fifth, thirteenth, and hundredth days have a direct relationship to this initial period. In turn, a successful hundredth day bodes well for the next year's first days, and from there, on to a rewarding career. And such success is well worth preparing for, because to work with young children is to be involved in the most exciting occupation in the world. Encouraging those who work with young children, as I now do, is the second most exciting.

1.
Preparing for the First Day

WHETHER you are teaching in a public or a nonpublic school, one of the first tasks needing your attention is the preparation of the classroom in anticipation of the children's arrival. Preparation generally includes:

1. arranging furniture, equipment, and materials
2. setting up learning centers or stations
3. borrowing, gathering, repairing, or purchasing furniture, equipment, and materials
4. planning and arranging teaching bulletin boards and displays
5. preparing lists of children's names, helper charts, an art box, and a welcome sign.

In both public and nonpublic schools, teachers are generally called back to work in the fall five to ten days before the children arrive. Rather than giving way to the feeling that the call to work is an intrusion into your summer holiday, look upon it as a great opportunity to get a head start in your classroom, childfree. Set aside feelings of excitement, fear, exhilaration, and anxiety; they use up precious energy needed elsewhere.

Close your door quickly. In the first few days of school, teachers may do a lot of visiting among themselves—which is fine for the experienced teacher who knows what tasks must be completed and how to allot the available time. The new teacher should not indulge. Minutes of social talk have a way of stretching into half hours and hours.

Room Arrangements

Make a quick survey of the room for size, furniture, and materials in drawers, on shelves, in cupboards, and in filing cabinets.

If you are in a public or nonpublic school with more than one kindergarten class, you may find it helpful to compare your furnishings with those of other kindergarten rooms. Occasionally teachers are willing to exchange various pieces of furniture. During the summer, the custodial staff often moves furniture out of the rooms as they are being cleaned, and furniture is often unevenly redistributed. Some schools have a policy of checking the condition of furniture, equipment, and materials at the close of the school term and making necessary replacements and repairs, which might include sanding, painting, or revarnishing; replacing missing pieces of wooden puzzles with plastic wood pieces which have been molded and painted; discarding some games or manipulative materials; combining sets with missing pieces to make a complete set or sets; or recommending purchase of new furniture, materials, and/or equipment.

Sometimes after the replacements and repairs have been made, the furniture, equipment, and materials are returned to the individual classrooms. In other cases, only the furniture will be returned, and all other materials will have been stored in a central location.

Most kindergarten classrooms have a small chair for each child; a larger chair for the teacher; a piano; tables for art and science activities, musical equipment, small manipulative materials, and library books; bookshelves; an easel; a block box; housekeeping furniture; a room-sized rug or several small rugs; and storage cabinets or closets.

If you discover a discrepancy in the amount of furniture in the different rooms, check with the other teachers or the custodian assigned to your section. Make friends with your custodian, who (along with the school secretary) makes your teaching job easier. Very often only the custodian may be aware of pieces of equipment and furniture stored away in various places in the school building. You may be able to use a particular piece of furniture or equipment for which another teacher has found no need.

Generally one or more meetings are called by the head teacher/director shortly after teachers are called back to work. At this time, you might appropriately bring up any questions you have about the furnishings of the classroom you will be using and about procedures for checking out, keeping, and returning materials from the central location. In addition, the school may have a policy not only for checking out art supplies, but also for the amount of material you will be allotted and for what particular length of time.

At the first meeting you won't think of all the necessary questions to ask, but you will think of them later. Keep a clipboard handy in your classroom on which you can jot down those questions as they come up; bring them to the next meeting. If the questions concern the safety or health of the children, don't wait. For example, if one of your work tables has a jagged edge that needs repair, bring it to the head teacher's/director's attention right away. Many of the questions you will record can often be answered by other teachers. It might be well to ask them first. For those questions still left unanswered, your head teacher/director would probably appreciate receiving them in written form—an informal note will do. School opening is a very busy time for everyone.

Placement of Furniture

Once you have explored your classroom, have some idea of how many children will be in the class, and have looked over the furniture at your disposal, your next task is to arrange the room, keeping in mind a rough idea of how many children will be working in what areas. Make preliminary drawings of possible room arrangements before moving any furniture. Following are three examples of possible room arrangements.

Room 1

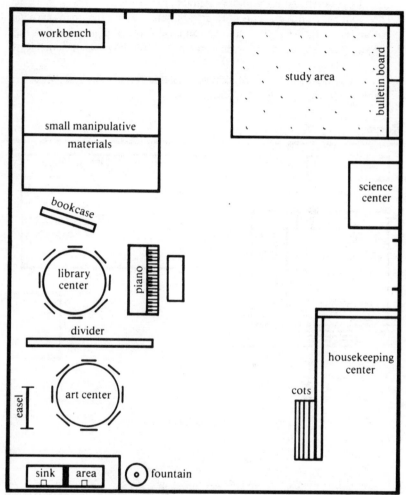

Rationale for Room Arrangements

Many times a teacher will be asked to defend a particular room arrangement. Any of the following responses could be offered:

1. This arrangement allows free flow and safe movement of children to and from the various centers of interest.
2. Quiet activities are separated from active and noisy ones.

3. The centers are set up to accommodate the optimum number of children who can work comfortably in any specific area.
4. The centers of interest provide all the children with enough activity, even though they differ in development and interests.
5. Materials are located in places close to centers where they will be needed so that the children can learn to use them independently.
6. The room has a large open area for large-muscle activity; the open space has within it an area where the children can meet for various activities. (A rug, the furniture arrangement, or lines marked by masking tape can delineate the meeting area.)
7. The room is arranged so that choices available for the day's activities are visible and inviting to the children.

Room 2

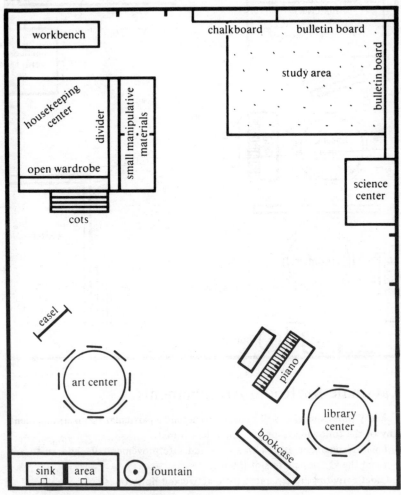

Teachers' Desks

Some teachers feel that a desk is necessary to provide a surface on which to keep important papers and to supply drawers for personal belongings. Other teachers feel that a desk takes up too much space in a kindergarten room.

Room 3

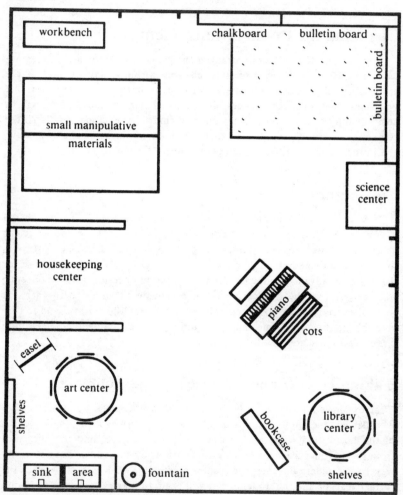

Even though the use of a desk is really a matter of personal preference, a note of caution might be sounded. Since many new teachers rely very heavily on their own experiences as children in school rather than on classroom techniques learned in college education courses, they might be prone to spend too much time behind their desks as they have seen former teachers do. It is difficult to fulfill a kindergarten teacher's role behind a desk.

I might suggest that a filing cabinet be used for important papers. A clothesline strung across the room can become a temporary sanctuary for an important paper handed to you in the middle of a very busy day.

If you do decide to have a desk, remember that many schools are open most of the day even when the teachers and students are elsewhere. A desk drawer offers no protection against anyone interested in rifling the contents of a purse or wallet.

Changing the Room Arrangement

If you find that the room arrangement which you have chosen does not work for you, make any necessary changes within a day or two. If the arrangement does work out satisfactorily, leave it for the first semester. If you then want to make changes, do so. By that time, the children will be able not only to adapt to changes but will find them exciting as well. At the beginning of school, stability in their room environment, in their schedule, and in their teacher provides feelings of security for young children.

Curriculum

If you have been given a curriculum guide with specific lessons in the various subject-matter areas or even a very general guide to follow, set it aside for the present time. Remember that the first few days of school are as exciting to the children as they are to you. These days are important not for making great advances in the children's acquisition or refinement of concepts, but for you and the children to become acquainted with one another—for you to set up rules for expected behaviors; to establish routines; and to provide the children with time and opportunities to get to know their classroom, classmates, and school.

Taking Over Someone Else's Classroom

Many times a teacher will be in the position of replacing another teacher who has left the job for one reason or another sometime during the year. One of the most difficult and frustrating tasks is to switch the children's allegiance from their former teacher to the new teacher. The new teacher will not in any way try to undermine the relationship or affection that existed between the former teacher and the students, but will begin to take certain steps to ensure an easy transition for both the children and herself or himself and will remember to practice patience in big measure. Some suggestions are:
1. Pretend for a little while that this is the very first day of school.
2. Arrange the classroom differently even if you like the arrangement the other teacher had.
3. Bring some personal items into the classroom so that it will feel like your classroom.

4. Prepare new charts, lists of children's names, helper charts, and a welcome sign.
5. Have a written message on the board telling the children your name and maybe one or two things you like to do.
6. Have some *very special* art and music activities and story books for the first day.
7. Follow the regular schedule.
8. When children say, "That's not the way our old teacher did it," have an answer ready. You might say rather matter-of-factly, "Is that right? People do things differently. This is my way of doing it."

If the new teacher provides an interesting learning environment for the children and practices good management procedures, most children will stop comparing the new teacher with their former teacher in a few weeks. Occasionally a child will persist. Try to be as patient as possible in dealing with him or her.

Setting Up the Art Center

Cover the table with newspaper. Some teachers feel that a round table promotes more conversation among the children. Set out large-size crayons and inexpensive paper. If eight children can fit at the table, set out that many sheets of paper and boxes of crayons ready to be used. If you do not have enough crayons, two children can share one box. All participants will at first need to be shown where to get more paper and where to place finished pictures.

Crayons

Any of the following reasons support the choice of crayons for use in an activity:
1. Crayons are the most familiar art medium known to children. Most children feel at home with crayons. The sight of something familiar in the room is reassuring.
2. Crayons require less supervision than other art materials. The teacher is bound to be busy for the first half hour of school, greeting children and parents. This activity easily keeps the earlier arrivals busy while he or she is occupied elsewhere.
3. If a child is already active at the art table, the teacher can ask him or her to include a newcomer, who can join the group without any specific instructions.
4. Productivity with different art media is less important on the first day than having children begin to develop social relationships with other children at the art table.

The Easel

The easel should be closed for the first day or until you have had time to introduce it. Although it is true that many children have used tempera paint by the time they come to kindergarten, it is also true that most kindergarten classes have some children who have not learned to paint without splashing on themselves, their classmates, and the room. This problem can be best taken care of when there is little commotion, and first days can be very hectic. (Chapter V, Art, offers more comments on how to introduce the use of the easel.)

Setting Up a
Small-Manipulative-Materials Center

Materials selected for inclusion at this center are intended to contribute to improvement in small-muscle dexterity, eye-hand coordination, visual perception, and problem-solving behaviors. The number of different materials provided will depend on the number of children who can work comfortably at the center at one time, and should allow for different abilities and interests. The center generally accommodates from six to eight children.

First-Morning Choices

Materials for the first day could include:
1. a rack of puzzles which range in difficulty, with several puzzles on the table ready for use
2. a Lego set with enough bases and pieces for two or three children
3. a set of balancing toys
4. a set of parquetry or a set of one-inch multicolored wooden cubes, and either teacher-made or commercially prepared designs for children to imitate.

Other Manipulative-Center Equipment

A wide range of interesting and educational materials is available through large companies which market children's toys and educational supplies. If possible, see equipment firsthand before purchasing. Check it for sturdiness, suitability for your group, and versatility of use.

Suitable equipment for this center might include: nesting materials (drums, cylinders, dolls, boxes), a miniature parquetry set with designs to follow, small chalkboards with chalk and erasers, a set of tiny farm or zoo animals, sequential puzzles, multicolored and multishaped beads with patterns to follow, toy hammer-and-nail set, Etch-a-Sketch, magic slates, Snap-N-Play blocks, Multi-Fit, Play Rings, Free Play Posts, play squares, play chips, color stacking discs, Fit-a-Size, Fit-a-Space, Fit-a-Square or Circle, Wonderforms, Playskool Color Cubes, large or small pegboard and pegs, Scope, tactile numeral blocks or alphabet, Rods and Counters, Bead Stair, flannelboard set, puzzles (4-15 pieces), lacing boards, learning-to-dress sets, small village, Mosaic, a box with cornmeal or salt in which children make designs, a magnetic board with numerals and letters, Rig-a-Jig, Lego, plastic shapes boards, Shapes Sorting Box, Intarsio, and Magnastiks.

Arithmetic Aids

Materials commonly called "arithmetic aids" deserve a place at this center only if you are aware of a limitation inherent in many such items. Many can be solved on a trial-and-error basis without any new mathematical learning taking place. Two examples found in many classrooms are:

1. A set of wooden pieces which show the numerals one through ten and a set of matching pieces which have one to ten objects drawn on them. The task is to fit matching pairs together.
2. A wooden board which has sets of wooden pegs with the corresponding numeral drawn near the correct number of pegs and a set of rubber squares which have from one to five holes. The child is required to place the squares in the correct position on the board.

However, if you sit near the child and ask questions as the child works with the materials, it is possible to find out what is happening in the child's mind and what the child knows about mathematics. You can then promote problem-solving behaviors.

Setting Up a Housekeeping Center

Equipment

Many schools purchase basic furnishings for this area, which should be open to the children on the first day of school. If money is limited and choices must be made, the underlined items would probably be most practical: table and chairs set; cupboard; refrigerator; stove; chest of drawers; crib or cradle; high chair; doll and doll buggy; ironing board and play iron; dishes; and pots, pans, and cutlery. You can enhance this area with articles picked up at garage sales, or items brought from your own home, or donated by parents. Real plastic dishes, adult-size cutlery, actual pots and pans, and kitchen gadgets are often more appreciated than toy ones. This center will also need dress-up clothes, which can include men's and women's shoes and hats; dresses, skirts, and purses; and jackets and ties. Small plastic mirrors and plastic cosmetic containers with powder or after-shave talc are popular. Empty food containers and plastic vegetables and fruit can fill the refrigerator or cupboard; and, on occasion, real foods can be added. Children enjoy cereals, crackers, vegetables, and fruit.

Items other than basic furniture will need to be changed occasionally. Additions such as toy plastic safety helmets similar to those used by construction workers, motorcycle or football helmets, baseball caps, used Halloween costumes, wigs or hairpieces, dancing skirts, and work boots or cowboy boots will bring renewed interest to the housekeeping center.

Commercially made furniture is costly, each piece costing about fifty dollars. If money is limited, buy fewer pieces but insist on quality. This furniture represents a good investment since it should last more than ten years. Reliable suppliers are Community Playthings, Creative Playthings, and Childcraft Education Corporation. (See Kindergarten Supply Sources in the Appendix for addresses.)

Limited Budget

If you have little or no furniture and not much money to purchase any, you can still create a successful housekeeping center. Garage sales constitute a great source for inexpensive items. Parents can be approached for small tables, bookshelves, record cabinets, small chests of drawers, plastic dishes, pots and pans, cutlery, and dress-up clothes. Check with the custodian for surplus furniture squirreled away in the school building. Painted wooden boxes and crates can substitute for crib, stove, cupboard, or shelves. Small chairs from the classroom can be used in the housekeeping center.

Limited Use

Set a limit on the number of children using this space at one time. The number will depend on the available space, but four has proven to be a reasonable limit in many situations. An easy way to help children remember the number limit is to post a drawing of that many children, with the numeral beside it, near the entrance to the center.

Setting Up a Woodworking Center

Safety

I suggest that this center be closed for the first few weeks of school, simply for the children's safety. Tools can provide wonderful experiences for children once you have taught proper use, but tools can be very dangerous in the hands of unprepared children.

After the initial excitement of the first few weeks of school has passed and the children have become accustomed to the room, introduce the workbench and tools on a gradual basis. You might introduce one tool each day, or choose to teach an interesting unit or set of lessons on Modern Tools or on Tools of Long Ago, or both. The woodworking area will be extremely popular once it is open. Since only two children can be accommodated at this center at one time, you will have to devise a fair method of ensuring all children the opportunity to work there. One way is to have all those who want to participate put their names in a hat; the sequence in which the names are pulled out determines their turn at the workbench.

Equipment

If money is available, purchase two real hammers of good quality, two real saws scaled to children, a brace and bit, a hand drill, a sturdy workbench and vise, and 1½- to 2-inch large-headed nails. Tools can be purchased at local hardware stores or from Childcraft Education Corporation or Community Playthings. (See Kindergarten Supply Sources in the Appendix for addresses.) If money is limited, buy the workbench, hammers, saws, and nails.

Miscellaneous items such as bottle caps, wooden wheels, Popsicle sticks, string, and glue can add interest. Free wood scraps can be obtained at building sites, lumber mills, or furniture manufacturing plants. Pine is preferable since it is soft enough for young children to use and resists splitting. Redwood scraps are also easy to work with. Avoid fir, which is widely available but frustrating to children.

Setting Up a Library Center

Books

If you are fortunate enough to have a library in your building, the task of creating a library in your classroom will be easier. It is always an enjoyable experience to select books to share with children. Later in the year, the children themselves can help choose books for the library center.

If you need help, talk to your school librarian; she or he is doubtless knowledgeable in the field of children's literature. Many excellent books are available for young children. (See Good Books for Children in the Appendix for a list of suggested titles and authors.)

For the first day, display nine or ten books on the library table and perhaps fifteen more on a nearby shelf or table from which children can make additional choices. Most of the books should be picture books, some with pictures only and others with many pictures and little text. Offer children information books as one choice also.

Library selections need to be changed often. Place books that have been read to the children at story time on the library table for those children who are interested in reliving the story experience.

Magazines

Magazines such as *Ranger Rick Nature Magazine,* published by the National Wildlife Federation, and *National Geographic World,* published by the National Geographic Society, make interesting additions to the library collection. (See Kindergarten Media Resources in the Appendix for addresses.) The children can enjoy the photographs and drawings even if they are unable to read the stories. You will need to spend some time introducing the magazines to the children and reading from them.

No School Library

If you do not have a school library, consult a public library. Most public libraries will loan enough materials to last about a week. Of course, librarians do expect that good care will be taken of the books loaned. You have the responsibility to discuss with the children the proper care of books or any other materials used in the room. This is another task to take care of very early in the year.

Garage sales are a source of inexpensive children's books. Parents sometimes will contribute books that their older children have outgrown. Paperback books are offered through the *See Saw News,* a division of Scholastic Book Services, at prices from thirty-five to seventy cents. (See Kindergarten Media Resources in the Appendix for address.)

Setting Up a Listening Center

The library table can also double as a listening center if you have access to a tape recorder and a listening station. A station includes sets of earphones and a master terminal which plugs into the tape recorder. You can easily make tapes of favorite stories and offer them for a self-chosen time activity. Merely provide multiple copies of paperback storybooks and record a signal on the tape to let children know when to turn the page, as they follow along in their books.

If a listening station is not available, a small record player with inexpensive records or used records from your own collection can be used for a listening experience.

Setting Up a Large Open Area

During self-chosen time this space can be used for construction with large and small blocks and for other activities with equipment not suitable for use on a tabletop, such as: sets of large and small trucks, airplanes, cars, or boats; Toymakers, zoo or farm animals; knights and a castle; cowboys; Tinker Toys; dinosaurs; Lincoln Logs; trains; a circus set; giant dominoes; drums; an Indian tent; a dollhouse with furniture and families; a puppet stage and puppets; and a village or harbor set.

The number of choices set out for the first day will depend on the number of children who might work in this area at one time. The number could vary from as few as three to as many as ten or more. If you offer too many choices, the area can become overcrowded, problems in social relationships can increase, children's ideas can be stifled for lack of adequate space, and children might wander from toy to toy without exploring the many possibilities offered by one set of equipment. An example of first-day choices could be:

1. large and small blocks and boards (offered every day)
2. dollhouse with furniture and family
3. Tinker Toys

4. a set of earth-moving equipment
5. a set of small cars.

This open area includes the regular gathering place for study, musical activities, language experiences, meetings, story time, and quiet games.

Quiet Game Area

Set aside a small space within the open area where two or three children can enjoy a card game, dominoes, checkers, or some other type of boxed game. (Chapter IV, Equipment, provides a list of boxed games.) A small rug can delineate the area. A Lotto game is a good first-day item to provide.

Setting Up a Science Center

Most kindergarten rooms have a table or tables set up on which collections of things can be displayed for children to observe and classify. Keep the collection small (six is a good number of items), as too many specimens can be overwhelming. Rocks, shells, butterflies, fossils, feathers, flowers, or seeds can be shown. Equipment suitable for independent experimentation by the children can also be made available; materials might include one of the following: a smelling or feeling box; a balance scale with a collection of objects for use; various sizes and shapes of magnets and an assortment of items on which to try the magnets; a container of water and various objects that the children can test for floating; or a terrarium with small inhabitants such as pillbugs, crickets, grasshoppers, katydids, earthworms, land snails, or a lizard or toad for observation. If you have a room pet, it could be kept near or on the science table.

Have several magnifying glasses handy. Good first-day activities include observing the room pet and examining a small collection of rocks.

Providing for Pets

Possible Choices

A hamster is a good pet for young children; it is large and slow enough for small children to handle. Some teachers prefer guinea pigs, gerbils, white mice, or hooded rats. Advantages and disadvantages exist for all of these pets. For example, white mice and gerbils move very quickly and very often get away from the children. White mice breed very often and have a strong odor if their nesting materials are not changed frequently. On the other hand, mice and gerbils are fun to watch. Gerbils require very little care and are practically odor-free. Guinea pigs are gentle and large enough for young children to handle easily, but unless you have outdoor accommodations or are willing to change the bedding materials very often, the odor in the room can become quite strong. Hooded rats make good pets and children seem to like them. They do have a strong odor, and many teachers are not very enthusiastic about handling them. Check state and school regulations before making a final decision.

Animals that Bite

Many teachers express the fear that children will be bitten by these small mammals. To avoid problems like this, the care and handling of any pet that will live in your classroom need to be discussed within the first hour of the first day of school. After the children have arrived at school, call a short meeting to talk about important rules and to give other information the children will be needing, such as safety rules, location of bathrooms and the drinking fountain, and choices of activity for the self-chosen time, which would follow. The safety rules should include information about the room pet; such information will keep the children from being hurt while handling the animal. You can begin by asking a series of questions:

- What might happen if you stick your finger into the cage? (You might get bitten.)
- Why might the hamster bite you? (He might think your finger is something to eat. He might think you're going to hurt him.)
- Is the hamster being mean? (No.)
- What would be a good rule to remember about the hamster? (Not to stick your fingers into the cage.)

Then say, "We will be talking about a safe way to take the hamster in and out of its cage a little later today. In a few days, you will be able to play with the hamster during self-chosen time. We want to be sure that the hamster will not be afraid and that no harm will come to you or it."

If you find that the animal you have purchased continues to try to bite after two or three weeks of careful handling, return it to the pet shop and ask for another. Some animals remain unmanageable.

Sources for Obtaining Animals

1. Science centers: Some cities have science centers or zoos from which animals can either be loaned to you or brought to the classroom by a resource person. If your city has such a center, sign up early.
2. Neighborhood children: Many times children have pets with more offspring than they will be allowed to keep.
3. Newspaper advertisement: A classified advertisement often brings good response.
4. Teachers: Let many teachers know that you are in the market for a small room pet. The end of school is probably the best time to obtain a pet from a teacher. Many do not want to keep their pets over the summer.

Arranging Bulletin Boards

A simple rule for teacher-made bulletin boards is that they be attractive, colorful, and useful for teaching. Most public-school classrooms have two to six bulletin boards of various sizes. Unfortunately, some rooms used as class-rooms in private schools are not equipped with any display space, and substitutes have to be found.

Small Boards

If your classroom has a small board near the front door, use it for children's name tags, which will be very useful the first day. Notes that the children bring from home or messages that need to go home with the children can also be pinned here. Keep tacks or straight pins handy at the top of the board. The name tags might relate to the study topic; for example, name tags cut in the shape of a hamster. As the children arrive, you can ask them to pick out their name tags. Offer help if it is needed.

A second small board can be used to display a simple helper chart, or the names of helpers arranged in some other way. Helpers are needed for certain tasks such as leading lines (if your school has children move about in this fashion), holding doors, helping with cots or mats, or helping in the cafeteria or at snack time. Some teachers use helpers to distribute and collect materials, take messages, greet visitors, straighten coat closets, or return materials to the library or office. You can make a simple chart that will assure each child an opportunity to experience the different roles.

Helper Chart

24 children, 6 pockets, 4 cards in each pocket

To change the chart, put Steve's card behind cards in Dalit's pocket, Dalit's card behind cards in Mort's pocket, and Mort's card behind cards in Steve's pocket.

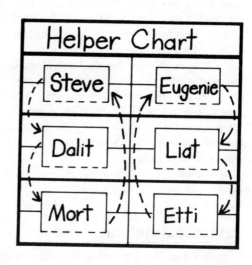

For the first two weeks of school, change helper chart daily. After that time, allow children to keep their "job" for one week. Change the chart at the end of the week and read the new list of helpers before the children go home on Friday.

Another bulletin board can be left empty at the beginning of the first day so that pictures from the art table can be displayed there as they are completed. Print the names of the children beside their work.

Study Boards

The study area will need a large board and perhaps one or two smaller boards to display drawings or photographs related to the study topic. First studies that have been very successful with Kindergarten children are: hamster, gerbil, guinea pig, mouse, rabbit, duck, parakeet, or turtle. If you have a room pet, it is a logical choice for a first study. In any case, choose one specific animal, rather than teaching birds, fish, or reptiles. There will be time for making generalizations later after the children know about a variety of animals.

The largest bulletin board can hold a large, simple outline drawing of the animal with all parts clearly delineated. The children can name the parts by either relying on their own past experiences or with the help of a set of teacher-made labels which match small tags near the various parts. For example, one label might be:

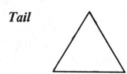

Tail

A red triangle big enough for the children to see appears near the word. This triangle matches a red triangle tag placed near the tail in the large drawing. If the child is able to find and match the label but cannot name the part, you read the label for the child and staple the label near the tail.

Use additional boards for more specific characteristics of your object of study. You might draw the children's attention to the fact that the number of toes varies from the back to the front feet, and that hamsters have special teeth for gnawing called incisors. Since a hamster is both a mammal and a rodent, use one small board to show pictures of familiar mammals and one for a collection of pictures of rodents. Include a picture of the hamster on both of these boards. The children will begin to see common characteristics among these animals.

It is important that the animal being studied be in the classroom for the children to observe. (See Chapter VII, Study Time, for a detailed unit on Hamsters.)

Additional Bulletin Boards

Empty boards can be filled with the children's art work completed in the first few weeks of school. Assure your class that all children will have a chance to show their art work sometime, and that after their art work is displayed for a few days, they will be able to take it home.

Children's Bulletin Boards

The children can occasionally be given the responsibility to construct bulletin boards related to study topics. Study boards can take shape as the children learn more about the topic. Holidays offer another opportunity to ask the children to decorate bulletin boards.

No Bulletin Boards

Don't despair about a lack of bulletin boards. If you supply your children with real objects and real experiences, their greatest needs for learning have been met. Having the hamster in the room is necessary while it is being studied; having pictures of hamsters is nice but not vital.

If your room has chalkboards, they can be covered with colored butcher paper and used as a backdrop for your drawings or pictures. Walls and sides of furniture can also be used. Remember that transparent or paper tapes can mar surfaces if left on them for long periods of time. Displays can also be made on the sides of large cardboard boxes or on cardboard made into sandwich boards.

Calendars

If teachers took time to think about the level of difficulty posed by a calendar, the choice would probably be made not to include one in the class-

Calendar 1

Date – September <u>6</u>

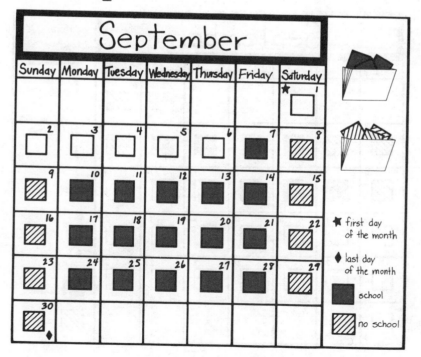

room. If you feel that you must have some system for marking or keeping track of the passage of time, construct a simple version of a calendar from which children can acquire the basic notion of days as calendar units, without the complexity of dates, per se.

Calendar 1: Cover the date numbers if they are prominent with white paper. Then cover each day's space with a square of colored paper. The paper pieces covering school days should be different in some way from those covering nonschool days. For example, school days could be covered with yellow squares and nonschool days with red. As each day passes, have a child remove one colored square from the calendar. On Friday, let three children each remove a square. (See example labeled Calendar 1.)

Calendar 2: The calendar can also be completed in reverse fashion; that is, by having a colored square ready to be placed on its proper space as each day begins. (See example labeled Calendar 2.) Using the second calendar, the children will be able to give information such as:

• There are five school days in a row; then I don't come for two days.
• There are more school days than days I don't come to school.

Calendar 2

Date — September <u>12</u>
Have squares ready to cover days

Other Needs for the First Day

1. A welcome sign on the door which might read:
   - Hello, my name is Mrs. Jackson. I'm glad that you have come.
   - Welcome to kindergarten. This is room 103.
   - Welcome to Brown School. .
   - Hello, my name is Mr. Williams.
   - This is your room. Welcome!
   - Good morning!
2. A list of the children assigned to your classroom posted outside your door.
3. A list of the children divided into smaller groups posted inside the room.

You may wish to choose names for the smaller groups, using neutral designations such as "red" and "blue" group rather than "redbirds" and "blackbirds." You can help the children remember the name of their groups in a number of ways. The name tags can be made out of paper of two colors. The names in the helper chart can be printed with colored ink pens, and each group posted on one side of the helper chart. A list of the entire class can be printed in two colors and posted on the front door—one group on the left side, the other on the right. A colored square of paper on the teacher's chair can indicate which group is to use chairs for that week's study time.

Collection of Money

Prepare a box to hold money that the children will bring to school to pay for lunches, snacks, special study trips, or weekly newspapers. Introduce the box at the first meeting on the first day. Remind the children to drop their money envelopes in the box when they first come into the room. Ask the parents beforehand to send money in envelopes marked with their child's name, the teacher's name, the amount of money, and the purpose for which it is to be spent.

Storage of Children's Art

Decorate a cardboard box with colored butcher, construction, or contact paper. Label it so that the children can identify it as the art box. Use pieces of cardboard as dividers, with children's first names entered in alphabetical order, to keep the children's art work separated. This method makes the weekly distribution of art an easy task. File art work daily rather than leaving it for long periods of time. Children can also learn to file their own art work.

Some teachers prefer to use ice cream dispensing cartons decorated by the children as individual storage bins for art work. However, cartons take up a lot of space and art work becomes crumpled in the cylindrically shaped containers. However, if you decide to use cartons, they can be obtained either free or at minimal cost at ice cream stores. The children can decorate them by making their handprints on them, after which you can apply a coat of clear lacquer over the whole surface. Make sure the children's names are printed on the cartons before applying the lacquer.

Home Visits

First days can be much easier if your school has a policy to have teachers make home visits before school opens. Teacher visitation in the homes of prospective students has many advantages. The children have an opportunity to see the teacher before school opens, which makes it easier for children to accept the home-to-school transition. The teacher has an opportunity to see the home environment of the children and to observe the interaction between parents and children.

If home visiting interests you, call the parents and make arrangements for short visits in the homes. Allow a maximum of thirty minutes for each visit and travel time between visits. Five visits can be fitted into a morning or afternoon without taxing your time or your ability to listen. Ask parents to have their child present for the first few minutes of the meeting. After the child is dismissed, you can ask pertinent questions about the child's growth pattern, health, abilities, interests, playmates, siblings, and former school experiences. Have parents explain discipline methods used in the home and any special information that needs to be shared that will affect the child's performance in school and also help you to understand the child better. The teacher can give the parent information about the program, schedule, pickup and delivery routines, safety rules, lunch or snack procedures, or needed materials. Some of this information can be on a form, so that the parent can retain it for reference throughout the year. If your class membership is complete, leave a copy of the list of children's names with each set of parents, if this is legal in your state. Such a list is helpful for parents interested in arranging car pools or inviting children over to play or to attend birthday parties.

Letters to Parents

About a week or ten days before school opens, you can send a letter to the parents giving the same kind of information that you would share on a home visit. This information would include:
1. amount of fees, if any
2. health and age requirements for entry into school
3. cafeteria prices for meals or snacks, and other information related to the lunch program; for example, restriction on the use of thermos bottles
4. a list of supplies needed by children
5. pickup and delivery suggestions
6. school opening date and hours of the school day
7. a request that any money brought to school by a child be put in an envelope clearly marked with the amount of money, the purpose for which it is to be spent, and the child's and teacher's names.

School Information Forms

Most schools have forms which parents are required to fill out and return before the opening of school, and teachers are often given these forms to keep in the room. All the following items of information could be helpful, but the laws in many states may prevent your asking some questions, at least on a form:

1. Child's full name and nickname
2. Child's address
3. Name of the parent or parents with whom the child lives; information about a divorce in the family and/or remarriage
4. Names and ages of siblings
5. Information about whether or not the child is adopted
6. Birthdate and birthplace of the child
7. Language spoken in the home
8. Past school experiences
9. Health record of the child; dates and places of immunization; childhood diseases child has had; any special health problems
10. Any special problems child has or has had
11. Names and relationship of persons to be reached in case of emergency if parents unavailable
12. Name of doctor and hospital in case of emergency
13. Names of two or three neighborhood children with whom child plays
14. Names of children from whom parents want their child separated.

2.
Schedules

T HE schedules which follow this short introduction are offered only as a guide. The needs of your group will dictate changes in any schedule which you adopt. Nothing is sacred about any schedule. It needs to serve you and the children, and flexibility is the key word to remember. At times, you will choose to change, shorten, lengthen, or eliminate an activity, particularly at the beginning of the school year. For example, in the first few days it might be necessary to break up the segment of time allowed for children's self-chosen activities. If children are having difficulty settling down or in using the equipment set out for this period, call a meeting to point out the available choices, to share art work already completed at the art table, to read several stories, or to introduce a finger play or two. Then allow the children to return to work.

Twenty minutes might have been allotted for a study period, but the children are restless and inattentive after only ten minutes have gone by. Their behavior is a signal to you to bring the lesson to a close or to make some changes in the activity.

If self-chosen time is over according to the schedule but the children are completely engrossed in activities which you feel are valuable learning experiences, let the activities continue.

If the children cannot sit still for a musical activity which requires that they do so, offer an alternate experience which allows the children to move about.

In many schools, you may have to adhere closely to the schedule at cafeteria or dismissal time. Also, if the playground area is shared by more than one teacher, you will have to honor an outdoor time schedule compatible with other teachers' needs.

Successful Scheduling

Some tips for successful scheduling are:
1. Have active periods alternate with periods in which the children have to stay reasonably still.

2. Remember that young children have a limit on the length of time that they can sit still or give complete attention. As the children get older and become more accustomed to the school routine, this time span will increase. A study in the first week might consume five minutes; by December, you may have increased study time to thirty minutes.

All of the following model schedules have been made up with the assumption that the teacher is responsible for the children all through the day and that there is no aide in the room. Although it is highly desirable to have able help in the room, most teachers are not that fortunate.

Half-Day Schedules

A. 8:30–11:30 a.m.

Self-chosen	8:30
Meeting	9:15
Cleanup	9:30
Bathroom	9:40
Study	9:50
Snack	10:10
Outside play	10:20
Rest	10:45
Music	11:05
Story	11:15
Dismissal	11:30

B. 8:00–11:30 a.m.

Self-chosen	8:00
Meeting and cleanup	9:00
Bathroom	9:15
Study	9:25
Snack	9:45
Outside play	10:00
Rest	10:30
Language activities	10:50
Music	11:05
Story	11:15
Dismissal	11:30

C. 8:00–12:00 a.m.

Self-chosen	8:00
Meeting	9:00
Cleanup and bathroom	9:15
Study	9:30
Snack	10:00
Outside play	10:10
Rest	10:45
Music	11:15
Language activities	11:30
Story	11:45
Dismissal	12:00

Full-Day Schedules

D. 8:00–2:00 p.m.

Self-chosen	8:00
Meeting and cleanup	9:00
Bathroom	9:20
Study	9:30
Outside play	10:00
Music	10:40
Lunch	11:00
Rest	11:30
Limited choices	12:15
Second study	12:35
Outside play	1:00
Story	1:40
Dismissal	2:00

E. 8:00–2:00 p.m.

Limited choices	8:00
Study	8:15
Outside play	8:45
Bathroom	9:15
Music	9:25
Self-chosen	9:40
Meeting	10:25
Cleanup	10:35
Story	10:45
Lunch	11:00
Rest	11:30
Limited choices	12:30
Second study	12:45
Outside play	1:05
Story or language activities	1:40
Dismissal	2:00

Full- versus Half-Day Programs

Some advantages of a full-day program are:

1. You have maximum leeway to lengthen, shorten, eliminate, or add activities if the need arises.
2. You have enough time to include two or three short instructional periods if such are desired.
3. You have increased opportunity to get to know the children in the class, bringing benefits to the children, their parents, and to you.
4. You can provide more learning experiences. The number of out-of-school field trips would probably increase.
5. Less paperwork is generated with one set of children than with two groups served by half-day programs.
6. You have time to fulfill specified goals, and still provide ample physical activities and enrichment.

Some advantages of a half-day program are:

1. You can eliminate attention to periods of the day (lunch, rest) which consume time but do not directly benefit the program. Your professional talents can be more fully utilized.

2. Children do not become fatigued as quickly as they do in a full-day program, particularly in the first few months of school.
3. You may remain fresher throughout the day. Two short programs are probably less fatiguing than working with one group all day.
4. You streamline your program, eliminating extraneous activities, so that each period of the short day brings the most benefits.
5. Fewer problems in classroom management arise.

Note: If no second class is scheduled, the afternoon period can be used for record keeping, gathering needed materials, preparing bulletin boards and other visual aids, previewing films, sharing ideas and problems with other teachers, calling parents or conferencing, doing library work, meeting with supervisors, or working with picture files.

Small-Group Study Times

If the self-chosen time is lengthened to seventy minutes, you can work with three groups of children, a group of eight children at a time, for fifteen-minute study periods. This kind of schedule can be undertaken after the children have become accustomed to their room, their classmates, and their teacher. Also, you will have introduced enough activities by that time for the children to pursue them independently.

This kind of arrangement has advantages and disadvantages. On the positive side, you have increased opportunity to individualize instruction, to interact with the children in smaller groups, and to monitor what is happening with each child. Discipline problems should lessen, since each child has a chance to participate more often; also, the study time is shorter. You may be able to cover more material if you do not have to take care of the few children who cannot function in a large group. With a shorter study time, the children will not tire as easily and should remain fresh and attentive throughout the study. Fewer materials might be needed. The larger group will have to become more independent and self-reliant while you are not available. You can develop a buddy system, whereby able children help children who are having problems.

Disadvantages of the small-group arrangement include a curtailment of the kinds of choices children are allowed in the classroom. Noisy activities have to be kept to a minimum. Certain art activities might not be offered. You miss the opportunity to interact with the children during self-chosen time, and you are not as likely to record anecdotal data concerning ongoing behaviors of the children. You have to repeat the same lesson three times.

Some classrooms combine both approaches. For some topics, large-group instruction is used; for others, small-group.

3.
The First Day

Greeting Parents and Children

THE first-day behavior of children varies greatly. While some children happily tell their parents good-bye and walk right into the room, others cling to their parents or insist the parents remain with them in the classroom. Occasionally a few children attempt to run away from their parents or out of the building. First-day parental behavior varies also. While some parents tell their children good-bye and confidently walk off, others are reluctant to leave. Some pretend to leave and then come back to peek through the door.

If home visits have preceded the opening of school, the problems will probably be minimal. Most of the children will be willing to leave their parents and come into the room. You can simply say good-bye to the parents and remind them of the place and time for dismissal.

You may be confronted with a crying child. Let me assure new teachers that in twelve years of kindergarten teaching, I have seen that in most cases the crying ends as soon as the parent leaves, or very shortly thereafter. The teacher needs to act in a firm but friendly manner when taking care of this problem. Insist that the parent leave, and take the child into the room. Since other children will be arriving, you can't and shouldn't remain with the crying child. Instead take the child to one of the learning centers where there are other children, introduce the newcomer and ask one child to tell what there is to do at that center. If the crying child does not want to participate, let him or her observe the other children. When you have time, check on the newcomer again to reassure the child that he or she has not been forgotten. If the child continues to cry and is disturbing the other children, lead the child to a quiet place in the room and make him or her comfortable. If you are still occupied greeting children at the door, you have no other choice but to leave the child there. In most cases, the child will be peeking between crying spells to see what is going on in the room. Sometimes it is best to let the child remain there until he or she feels like moving.

The children who are eager to become involved in the classroom can be asked or helped to find their name tags and shown some of the choices they can make. Children who are already occupied at various learning centers can be asked to introduce the activity to other children.

The First Meeting with Children

As soon as all or most of the children have arrived, ask them to come to you for a short meeting. Take the roll and then introduce *the signal* (use only one signal) that you will be using to get their attention. The first meeting will need to include information about bathroom and water locations, the names and locations of the various learning centers, choices for self-chosen time, any specific rules that you may have concerning equipment in the room, and safety rules. If you do not have adequate closed storage and have to use open shelves to house toys, you may have a rule that toys are not to be taken from the shelves unless you have given permission to do so. Safety rules could include information about the room pet, paper cutter, and fan, about the allowed limit for height of constructions, about throwing equipment, or about leaving the room without your knowledge. Before dismissing the children, remind them of available choices and of the signal and tell them you are glad that they are in your room. If you think it would be worthwhile, take a tour of your room so that the children can see the various learning centers and the bathroom locations.

Self-Chosen Time

Although the time that is devoted to self-chosen activities will vary from school to school and even room to room in the same school, children's behavior in this situation will be more alike than different. For the most part they will be quiet and shy during the first couple of early-morning free-choice times. Children use this time to "size up the teacher"—to make certain judgments about the kinds of activities that will be offered and the kinds of limitations that will be set. Limitations are particularly important. In the introduction, I suggested that what you do in the first few days and weeks of school will affect children's behavior and the program for the whole term. Your role in the room is of *extreme* importance, especially at the beginning of school. If you have set a limitation on the way a piece of equipment may be used, for instance, it is important that you insist right from the beginning that the limitation be honored.

Some children will become actively involved, while others will wander around the room before settling on an activity. Some children will have difficulty making choices, but they usually make up a small percentage of the class enrollment. The children who resist your efforts to bring them into a group or an activity need a period of time just to watch you, the other children, and the activities in the classroom before venturing out on their own. However, if this behavior persists day after day, contact the parents. Perhaps they can give you additional information which might be of help. Some strategies will have to be worked out to help such children to become part of the group.

You may find it necessary to divide the self-chosen time into smaller segments. If many of the children seem to be having difficulty settling down, call a meeting after fifteen or twenty minutes have elapsed and use it to teach several simple finger plays or a song. Have a story or two ready to share with children. Remind them of the choice of activities and release them again.

Final Meeting Before Cleanup

Let the children know that this is the meeting before cleanup so that they will know that they will not be returning to play. Share the art work completed at the art center, any large or small block constructions that are still standing, and design work done at the small-manipulative-materials center. Review the finger plays or songs taught at one of the shorter meetings.

Cleanup

Compliment the children on their activities and tell them about the choices that will be available for the next self-chosen time on the following day. Then discuss the putting away of all equipment so that you can go on to the next scheduled period of the day. No matter what procedure you devise for cleaning up the room, be prepared for it to be rather disorganized. Don't be disheartened; it will improve.

A number of ways exist to assign tasks to children. You can touch each child's head as you announce what his or her "cleaning job" will be. You can ask one child to be the block helper and to pick three helpers, and then continue to name leaders for specific jobs until all tasks have been assigned. You can ask for volunteers for specific jobs. One group can take care of tables and the other group the floor area. Some teachers just announce that it is cleanup time and ask the children to put things away. Before releasing any children to clean the room, remind them about equipment locations and ask them to come to you after the room is back in order. After some time goes by, you will begin to know your children very well. You will know whom to ask to be a big block helper, who does a very careful job cleaning up the art center, which children know where equipment goes, and which ones do not like to help with cleanup.

When the room is straightened up and the children have gathered around you, send a few at a time to the bathroom and others for drinks. Once the cleanup becomes routine, children can make their own choices about using the bathroom and getting drinks before settling down for study time.

First Study

I had suggested earlier that curriculum guides be set aside for the first few days of school. However, the first day's schedule can include a short study, one that is related to young children's interests. Even though this study is short, study time is thus established in your routine from the very first day of school.

Seating Arrangements

If you have a large rug, have the children sit around the three outside edges facing the study boards. If the group is too large, divide the children into two groups and let one group sit on chairs and the second group on the rug in front of the chairs. Alternate groups the next week. If there is no carpet, use paper tape to outline the study area for the first couple of weeks or until the children have become accustomed to the seating arrangement.

Study Sample for the First Day

We will assume that the hamster was introduced as the room pet at the very first meeting of the day. Bring the hamster in its cage to the study area. Children take a little time to settle down. Instead of waiting for all of the children to be quiet, start a finger play or song, As you continue, most children will settle down to listen or to join in. If you play a musical instrument, use it; if you don't, pick up some finger cymbals, rhythm sticks, or a tambourine. (Many moments during the day you will need a two- or three-minute activity to bridge the time and make the transition from one activity to another proceed smoothly. These short activities help to bring the children together as a group and to focus attention on you. See Transitional Activities in the Appendix.)

Once you have the children's attention, remind them that the hamster will not be frightened when you take it out if they will keep their voices low and keep their hands by their sides. Ask them not to make any sudden movements. Take the hamster out and place it in the middle of the study area. If any children seem frightened, show them how to make a wall with their hands by keeping all of their fingers together and how to push the hamster back into the center of the area. Compliment children who remember the rules. Let the children know that their first task is to observe the hamster. After a few minutes, pick up the hamster. Walk around so that any child who wishes to can stroke the animal from the back of its head to the tail. Replace the hamster in its cage and set it aside. Then ask:
• Can you tell me one thing about the hamster?
Let as many children as possible answer, even if their responses are repetitive. Children might volunteer that it is brown, small, looks like a mouse or a rat, has two ears, black eyes, whiskers, short tail, moves low to the ground, moves quickly, has four feet, and is furry. Your next questions will be based on the information that has been volunteered. If children seem reluctant to answer, ask:
• What kind of covering did you see on the body?
• How did it feel?
• What color is the fur?

- How many feet did you see?
- What can you tell me about its tail?
- Do you know any animal that is about the same size as our hamster?
- How did the hamster move?
- Someone said that the hamster reminded them of a rabbit. Can you tell me why?
- How did the hamster use its front paws?
- When it yawned, did you notice if it had any teeth? How did they look?
- What do you like about the hamster?

The objectives of this first lesson are to provide an opportunity for the children to improve their observation and classification skills and to have an enjoyable experience.

As the lesson comes to a close, either because the goals have been attained or because the children can no longer give adequate attention, remind the children that the next study will be about the hamster's special characteristics. Compliment them for contributing to the study.

Successful Study Times

Some tips for successful study times—first day and every day—are:

1. Before you start, make sure that the children are not crowded and that everyone can see the study boards or exhibits.
2. Be sure the room temperature is comfortable.
3. Take care of special problems before you start, such as children who have difficulty hearing or have visual problems, children who cannot seem to sit still, children who cannot sit near each other without chatting all the time, children who cannot keep their hands to themselves; a crying child. (Suggestions for handling these different situations are found in Chapter IX, Room Management.)
4. Precede the study time with an active period, a period in which the children have an opportunity to move about freely. (Cleanup is an active time.)
5. Choose materials which will challenge the children but which will, at the same time, provide learning opportunities for all of the children.
6. When applicable, let each child have his or her own set of materials.
7. Use real objects if possible.
8. Provide a variety of study topics.
9. Keep the lesson moving.
10. Keep the study time short, continually monitoring the length of time the children are able to give their attention without becoming tired or disinterested.

Snack Time

If the snack is to be eaten outside, remind the children to use the bathroom if it is necessary before leaving the room. Count the children. Have them pick up their snacks and follow you to a prechosen outdoor location. Insist that the children stay with you even if some of them finish their snacks before the others. As they eat, remind them that outside play is next and that some things need to be talked about before you can release them. Suggested snacks for young children include an apple, grapes, several crackers, a banana, or a half sandwich. Since water is available on most playgrounds, the children usually do not need to bring a drink.

Outside Play

A few simple steps taken before releasing the children will bring benefits both to you and them. Make a count before you leave the snack area. Insist that the children stay with you until you are ready to release them. Walk the boundaries of the play area so that there will be no misunderstanding as to where they are to play. Discuss safety rules for any equipment found on the play yard. Remind them of the signal which you will be using to call them back together.

Once the play period begins, your responsibility is to watch the children. Socializing with other staff members is fine if it is done without interfering with the safety of the children. Make another count before returning to the classroom.

Equipment

Play equipment varies from school to school. The ideal play area for young children would include an open grassy area, a gentle hill, and versatile equipment, limited only by children's ability to imagine the ways in which it may be used. Sadly, some teachers will find only a concrete or asphalt area available to them for the children's play space. It is possible to enhance any play area by adding inexpensive items such as a sandbox, tire swings, a tire wall, tires for rolling, monkey swings, rope ladders, boxes, buried stumps, barrels, boards and blocks, balls, ropes, and small toys from the classroom.

Injured Children

Even when you fulfill your role on the playground, children will get hurt. When an accident occurs, try to keep cool. Carry a few Band-Aids and some paper tissues in your pocket for minor scrapes. If you are alone on the playground and the injury seems serious, signal to the children to meet and take them all inside to get emergency care for the injured child. Occasionally a parent will have to be called to pick up a child. If you are not alone on the playground, signal to the children and bring them to another teacher; tell them that you must leave with the injured child for a few minutes and that their needs will be taken care of by the other teacher.

Music for the First Day

Procedure

Pick out a song or two that you like. If the children tell you that they know it, that's fine. Tell them you are glad because now they can sing along with you and help teach it to the other children. But be prepared to sing solo anyway; sometimes when children say that they know a song, they actually mean that they know a line or two or perhaps the chorus. Sing the first verse through with no musical accompaniment. Face the children as you sing. Have the children sing it with you a second time. Teach the chorus and then go back and have the children sing the first verse and chorus with you. If you find the children responsive, go on with the second verse. Then sing the song through once again. If the song has a number of verses, some can be taught the second day after reviewing those already introduced. If the song is very short, teach a second song also, if you like. A simple song like "Skip to My Lou" is an appropriate choice for the first music time, and it can be used for a variety of musical experiences later on. If there is time, include some simple finger plays. (Suggestions for finger plays for the beginning of the year are found in the Appendix under Finger Plays.)

The music lesson can take place in a special location, the study area, or outside. Once again, make sure that the children are comfortable before starting. If the children seem restless, include an activity which allows them to move about and then return to your original plans. (See the section in the Appendix titled Transitional Activities for ideas.) On the second day, review the finger plays and songs already taught and introduce one or two new ones.

Lunch Time

The length of the school day varies from school to school. Some schools have only morning programs, while others combine school and day care into a full day's program. In a half-day program, lunch is generally not served. Some schools that have full-day kindergartens begin their six-hour program on the very first day of school. Others allow one or two weeks before requiring the children to remain at school all day.

In schools which provide lunch, procedures will vary from serving the food cafeteria style to having the children served at small tables.

If you find yourself at a school which allows several weeks before the children stay at school for lunch, time can be taken during the shorter day to "practice cafeteria." Housekeeping furniture, dishes, and utensils can be used for demonstration and practice. It is wise to end the study with a few simple rules about lunch procedures. Try generating rules by asking the children specific questions. For example:

• How would you feel if your neighbor took food off your plate?
• Why is it not a good idea to exchange food, milk cartons, or eating utensils?

- What would be a good thing to do if you feel like coughing?
- What's a good thing to do when there's a new food on your plate?

Make a chart with a title to record the rules you devise. Display it in the room. Some appropriate titles might be:
- IT'S FUN TO EAT LUNCH TOGETHER
- LUNCH-TIME LIMERICKS
- WE KNOW IT'S IMPORTANT TO:
- RHYME TIME ABOUT LUNCH TIME

Try to express all rules in a positive way. Some of the rules could be:
- We use our own forks, spoons, and straws.
- We eat food only from our own plates and drink milk from our own milk cartons.
- We leave the table only when we're excused.
- We try new foods.
- We visit with each other using low voices.

An example of a more lighthearted approach for a chart on rules is:

Lunch time, lunch time,

It can be a fun time;

Time to eat and time to meet,

Time to remember to stay in your seat.

What's yours is yours,

What's mine is mine;

If we remember the rules,

We'll have a fine time.

The cafeteria can be visited the first time simply to point out its location and the tables at which the children will be eating. A second visit can include walking through the line and having the children sit at the tables. If you have divided your children into two groups, the groups can sit at opposite sides of the tables. The children who will be cafeteria helpers can also be shown where they will sit. A third visit can include bringing snacks to the cafeteria, placing them on trays, walking through the lines, and sitting and eating at the table.

If you send a note home requesting parents to send money to purchase milk, the children can practice the purchasing procedure and open the milk carton at the lunch table. You can also bring a milk carton to the room to demonstrate how to open it. A discussion of a safe way to carry the tray might avert some spills. Since some children become anxious when faced with a new situation, these practice days can make the "real thing" go smoother and help to alleviate any anxieties children might have.

If your school begins a full-day schedule immediately, you can take some steps that will be of help. First, ask the cafeteria manager if it would be all right to bring the children five or ten minutes early for the first few lunch times. In addition, delete the study-time topic for the first day and replace it with a study centered around "going to the cafeteria." Have a short talk about what this experience will be like and what the children will be doing. Include a visit to the cafeteria. Take the children through the line and to the tables. Demonstrate the opening of a milk carton. Ask the cafeteria helpers to pretend to do their tasks.

Using Helpers

Let the two room leaders lead the children to the cafeteria and allow one group at a time to proceed through the line. Help the children to get their trays, milk, and straws, and to pay the cashier. Show this first group where to sit and then go back to help the second group. When all the children have been seated, move the cafeteria helpers to the head of the tables so that they will be close to the area where they will be helping the other children. The milk helper can empty any milk left over from lunch and replace the empty cartons on the children's trays. The paper helper can pick up anything made of paper and put it in a trash container. The child carrying the tray can then give it to the adult cafeteria helper.

The two children who have been designated as lunch room leaders can straighten chairs, clean the tables, and then take their places near the exit doors to lead the children back to the room. Cot or mat helpers can follow the leaders so that they will be ready to help the children with their cots or mats.

Ask six children at a time to get up from the tables and to stay in a designated spot after putting up their trays—until all the children have left the tables.

After a month or so, the children can be allowed to return to their rooms, pick up their cots, and prepare for rest independently. I have found that there are far fewer problems in following this procedure than in having young children wait and then return in lines to their homeroom.

Note: Even with practice, the lunch routine will be hectic for the first couple of weeks. It will improve.

In some schools, sympathetic principals loan aides or older students for the first week to help kindergarten children and teachers at lunch time. Some parents are willing to act as helpers also.

Rest Time

Have a short meeting near the cots where you can demonstrate a safe way to pick up a cot, carry it, and put it down. Let a child or two demonstrate also. Let four children at a time line up to get their cots. When all the children are on their cots, tell them what story they will be hearing. If you take this time to relax also, you will find that the children will settle down more quickly. Some strategies for taking care of children who are not able to lie quietly on their cots are to stroke their backs for a few minutes or whisper a message in their ears. Sitting close to a child will sometimes encourage the child to relax. Choose story records that you have listened to and know are appropriate. Familiar stories, short in length and told clearly, are good choices for rest times in the first few weeks. You can also read to children as they rest. Tell them that the pictures will be shared when they get up.

When rest time is over, have the cot helpers put away their cots first. Call children up two or three at a time and remind them how to carry their cots in a safe manner. After a month or so, choose a child each day to call the children up from rest. Since the child will usually have been selected because he or she is a good rester, there will be incentive for other children to be good resters also.

Suggested Activities for a Second Study

The following suggestions can be used in a full-day program, which would allow a second study time. They can be applied the first day or other days.

Mathematics Lesson

New language introduced: collection, set, member of a set

Collect an assortment of objects from the classroom and place them on a large white sheet of paper in front of the children. Include objects of different sizes, shapes, and textures. This collection might include any of the following items:

small cars, boats, or trucks
boxes of different sizes and shapes
plastic geometry tools
money
crayons
scissors
nails
pencils
brushes
wheels

Choose one item and place it on a second sheet of paper. Be sure that all children can see it. Ask a child to find something from the large collection of objects which resembles your choice in some way. After the child has made a selection, ask him or her to give a reason or reasons for the choice. Be careful not to prejudge the accuracy of the choice. Although many children will classify objects by color or shape, just as often a child will see a relationship between objects which is not readily apparent to an adult's eyes. Have the child name the set. If the child is unable to do this, you name the set. Example: "This is a set of *things you can see through.*" Let other children add additional members to the set. A variation of this task is to let a child start a new set and let other children add new members. After a new set has been made, pick up each object in the set and say, "This object is a member of the set of *things you can see through.* Can you name or show me another member?" If you feel that the children understand what has been presented, introduce a game which will allow more practice of the new language. Let a child make a set of objects, whisper the name of the set in your ear, and then allow other children to guess the name of the set. The reason for telling the name to you is to check on the reasonableness of the name, to save a child any embarrassment, and also to ensure that the child not forget or change the name if someone makes a correct guess.

You can also begin the lesson by placing two or three objects together and saying, "I will call this set of objects *things that are green.*" Then remove the set, make a new set, and name it.

Compliment the children as they work and when the learning sequence is over. You can say such things as:

- I never would have thought of that.
- You are right.
- You knew exactly what to do.
- You are good thinkers.
- This lesson is moving along very quickly because all of you are helping.
- I like the way you are working.
- You must be feeling very good about yourselves today.

End the lesson if you see the children's interest lagging, even if you feel that your goals for the study time have not been accomplished. Children learn best when they're not fatigued and their interest is high. Leave the children with some information about the next study's activities. For example, "Tomorrow, each of you will have your own collection of objects to make into sets. Maybe we will play our guessing game again tomorrow."

Let me suggest one question to use in evaluating any set of materials used to teach mathematics to young children. Are ample opportunities provided in the sequence of lessons for children to build meaning for the concepts which are introduced? For example, before children are expected to deal with the symbol 5, do they have a firm grasp of fiveness? Do they know it as sets of zero and five, five and zero, one and four, four and one, two and three, and three and two? Do they know that five things are fewer than six things, but more than four things?

Language Activity

You can order a weekly newspaper which will be mailed directly to your school. Two such newspapers are the *Weekly Reader Surprise,* published by Xerox Publications, and the *Let's Find Out* series, published by Scholastic Book Services. (See Kindergarten Media Resources in the Appendix for addresses.) Both of these newspapers are geared toward young children. Subscriptions are inexpensive, and each child receives a copy. The teacher receives a teacher's edition. The children do not have to be able to read to use these papers; language development seems to be the main objective of both publications. New concepts are introduced in ways that are interesting to children. Listening and sharing skills can be improved through the use of these materials.

If the school or parents are not able to pay for the cost of a newspaper, you can derive similar benefits from materials you have prepared or from activities you provide for the children. Large pictures and book illustrations can be used to promote discussion. If you choose to use a large picture as the basis for class discussion, be sure to ask a variety of questions—questions that call for different levels of thinking. The lowest level asks children for a simple statement of fact. For example, "What color sweater is the child wearing?" Questions which will elicit higher levels of thinking are often open-ended questions, for which there are no right or wrong answers. Some examples would be, "What would you have done if you had found yourself on an island all alone?" or "Why do you think the child decided to help the giant?"

Know your children. Be sure to ask the right question of the right child. Once you have asked a question, stay with the child until closure occurs and the child has had a successful experience. The children will all learn from each other as discussion takes place.

Language Systems

Many oral-language systems are available from a variety of publishers. Although all are called oral-language systems, some more closely resemble readiness and/or beginning reading programs seen in the first grade. Some systems include many manipulations for the teacher's and children's use. If you are considering using an oral-language system, keep one important idea in mind: Review how young children acquired the language that they brought to school at the age of five. For the most part the vast storehouse of available words was built up over time with the support and guidance of the child's parents or parent-substitute as the child interacted with real things in the environment. With this in mind, consider very carefully whether a "kit" can serve as the equivalent of experiences in which the child hears, sees, touches, smells, and tastes "real" things in the classroom, supported and guided by a teacher who understands thoroughly how young children learn best! Oral language development takes place all day in a good kindergarten environment.

Special Movies

The second study time can be used to show a film related to the study topic, music, art, or literature. Try to preview films before sharing them with the children. Keep notes on what the film contains and how you rate the film. If you do not have time to preview all the films you share, check with other experienced teachers for information and ratings on movies they have used with young children.

Most public schools have film libraries from which films can be ordered and kept by the teachers for a number of days. Some public libraries also have a film library. Other sources for films include universities and colleges, professional teachers' groups, commercial companies, and state parks and wildlife departments.

Introducing a Musical Instrument

You might spend time examining a ukulele or guitar—finding out how many strings each instrument has, how the strings are held in place, what happens when a finger is placed on a particular fret and the instrument strummed, and how it sounds when strings are tightened or loosened. Rhythm-band instruments can also be introduced during one of these study times.

Introducing Some of the School Staff

Take a walk with the children to meet the principal, the office staff, librarian, cafeteria help, and school nurse. Alert these people before the visit.

Exploring the School Building

Locate the important places such as the office, the library, the art and music rooms, the first-grade classrooms, the gymnasium, and other kinder-garten rooms. This is an appropriate time to talk about behavior in an emergency situation. For example, what should a child do who becomes separated from the group? Many times the answer to this question will come from the children in your group:
- Tell any grown-up you see that you don't know where your teacher is.
- Ask an older child where the office is or to show you where your classroom is.
- Ask a custodian to help you find your teacher.

Exploring the Neighborhood

Establish a few simple rules before leaving your room. For example:
- We stay with the teacher.
- We hold our partner's hand.

Take a short study walk in the neighborhood. Walk near the middle of the group. You can choose one of a number of different objectives:
- *Color Identification.* Take with you four-inch squares of colored construction paper (red, blue, yellow). Show the children the red square and tell them you will be looking for things that are red. Ask them to raise their hand when they see something red. Change the color after a few minutes.
- *Identifying Living Things.* Establish with your children at least one characteristic of living things. (They move, they grow.) Take a clipboard with you and jot down things the children identify as living. You can encourage further discussion when you return to the classroom. Later you may wish to divide this list into two classifications: plant and animal.

Story Telling and Drawing

Tell a favorite folk tale and have the children draw either a character from the story or illustrate one thing that happens in the story.

Self-Portraits

Ask the children to draw a picture of their faces on one side of the paper and a full-figure self-portrait on the other side. Date the pictures and keep them in the children's files for sharing with parents, and for comparing to results of a similar request made later in the year.

Sharing of Family News

Tell about the members of your family and show pictures of them. Let children who wish to share tell about their families also.

Sharing of Summer Experiences

Relate one experience that you had during the summer. Let those children who wish share some information about what they did or about a place they visited during the summer.

Introducing an Inside Game

Introduce a game suitable for indoor playing. There will be rainy days for which you will need a ready supply of such activities. (See the section titled Indoor Games for Rainy Days in the Appendix.)

Story Time

Carefully choose the literature that you plan to share with the children. So many wonderful books are available for young children today that this task will not be difficult. Have two or three books ready to read on the first day. These will be picture books—books with lots of pictures and few words. Sit in a rocker or a child's chair and practice holding the book with one hand placed at the bottom of the book, grasping both pages and holding them open for the children to see. Occasionally move the book to the other hand. Be aware of the level at which you are holding the book. When the children are seated on the floor, you'll need to hold the book just a little higher than their eye level. Make sure that the children are not looking into any glare as you read. Some teachers learn to read upside down; if you can do this, hold the book directly in front of you, chest level. Some suggestions for appropriate first-day choices are (See Good Books for Children in the Appendix for more complete information on these and other books.):

Asbjornsen, *The Three Billy Goats Gruff*

Bridwell, *Clifford, the Big Red Dog*

Ets, *Gilberto and the Wind*

Flack, *Angus and the Cat*

Flack, *Angus and the Ducks*

Gag, *Millions of Cats*

Hillert, *The Three Bears*

Keats, *Peter's Chair*
Keats, *Whistle for Willie*
Krauss, *The Carrot Seed*
Krauss, *The Growing Story*
Langstaff, *Over in the Meadow*
Lionni, *Inch by Inch*

Minarik, *A Kiss for Little Bear*
Potter, *The Tale of Peter Rabbit*
Slobodkina, *Caps for Sale*
Tworkov, *The Camel Who Took a Walk*

As you finish reading the last story, tell the children that the books that have been read will be placed on the library table. The library center will be one of their free choices during self-chosen time in the morning.

Dismissal Time

Different dismissal procedures are followed in various schools and school districts. Some schools request that the parents come to the classroom or play yard to pick up their children. Others dismiss the children at the classroom door. If children are picked up by car, it is important that you discuss safety procedures with the children before they leave the classroom. A good time is after story time and after you have shared announcements or special messages with the children. You can ask questions which will lead the children into thinking about and verbalizing appropriate behaviors at dismissal time. It's often wise for you to say, "Please stay close to me until I see your mother or father. I will put you into your car." First-day dismissals are rather hectic, just like first-day cleanups, but they will improve. The main rules that you want the children to agree to are all related to safety; for example:

- We do not run into the street.
- We wait until the teacher puts us in our cars.
- We leave only with the people who regularly pick us up.
- We go home with another child only if a note has been brought to our teacher.
- If we walk, we go right home.

Introducing New Equipment

In the first few weeks of school, you will be introducing materials that will be added to the supply from which children will make choices. Introduce new equipment by questioning the children about how they think it may be used, rather than telling them your ideas. Not every toy or piece of equipment will need to be introduced. Occasionally you will want to set out something new without explanation; at the meeting before the cleanup of the room, the children can share ideas as to the many ways they found to use it. Respect for all school equipment is important and needs to be discussed, since you will be bringing many things into the room either from your own or from other people's collections. Others will be unwilling to lend their treasures if the word gets around that your children do not know how to respect other people's property.

By taking time to introduce new equipment, you endow the item with a special value. Many times, children will not choose or even notice certain materials until you have brought them to their attention. If the care of equipment is discussed, the equipment tends to have a longer life span in the classroom. The children will understand that there are limitations as to how a piece of equipment may be used.

Other Hints for Successful First Days

1. Keep in mind that first-day behaviors are often atypical for most children.
2. Remember to be friendly, kind, clear, and concise about the few important rules that are set down on the first day. If they are truly important, the same rules will apply the first as well as the last day of school. Set down other rules as they are needed.
3. Have a number of various kinds of short activities in reserve for the first day. You may find a rainy day greeting you on your very first day of teaching. (Use some of the suggestions found in the Appendix, in the sections on Finger Plays, Transitional Activities, and Indoor Games for Rainy Days; Chapter VI, Music.)
4. Remember that the children's first-day impressions of you can be lasting ones. Though this thought may be very difficult for a new teacher to accept, it is much more important that the children respect you as their teacher than that they like you. I am not saying that it is unimportant whether or not the children like you, but I advise against the feeling that many new teachers have—that getting the children to like them is the first priority. If you provide the kind of environment in which young children flourish, there is no doubt in my mind that the children will not only respect you, but will like you as well.

4.
Equipment

MANY new teachers will be asked to order equipment for their room. Since money is usually not available every year, you may have to live with your choices for some time. There are a number of ways to seek help. Talk to experienced teachers who have good reputations for work with young children. Ask what equipment they would order if they had a limited amount of money. Information gained from an experienced teacher might include the versatility, life span, and value of a particular item, and the general response of children to it. Browse through catalogs from established companies and, if possible, visit their showrooms. Occasionally school districts will have companies display their merchandise locally. Visit toy stores to see the equipment. Be wary of advice from toy-store owners, since their experience with actual use of the toys is generally limited. Their only experience may be from their own child or grandchild. Equipment to be used by a classroom of active youngsters has to be in a special category of sturdiness. As a general rule, wooden toys outlast most other toys. Some sturdy metal trucks and cars also have a long life. If money is limited, buy a few sturdy toys and augment these expensive items with dime-store boats, cars, cowboys, or dinosaurs, which can be replaced with only a small outlay of money.

Well-made wooden trucks should have a life span of about fifteen years. Hollow wooden blocks and smaller solid blocks of varying shapes and sizes are the most expensive investments. Take great care in placing an order for these items. If they are carefully chosen, the life span of hollow blocks should be about fifteen years and that of unit blocks even longer.

Classroom Equipment for 20-25 Children

General

Hollow Blocks—Community Playthings: ½ set (14 squares, 8 double squares, 8 half squares, 2 ramps, 4 long blocks, 4 short blocks), plus 10 double squares

Unit Blocks—Childcraft: ¼ set (190
    pieces), plus 8 large columns, 6
    large switches, 20 double units,
    4 ellipses, 4 curves
Clip-on Wheels—Creative Playthings:
    6 pair
Large trucks (wooden and metal):
    earth-moving truck, moving van,
    farm truck, fire truck, lumber
    truck, tow truck
Small vehicles (wooden): jeep, pick-
    up, police car, ambulance, station
    wagon, taxi
Large and small wooden boats and
    ships
Large and small cars
Wooden train set

Tinker Toys
Doll house, furniture, and families
Lego
Cowboys
Wild animal set
Farm animals, barn, fences
Block bin
Lincoln Logs
Village and/or harbor set
Toy Maker
Dinosaurs
Knights and castle
Circus set
Miniature traffic signs
Set of airplanes

Small Manipulatives

Sequential puzzles
Puzzles, 6-18 pieces
Magnasticks
2 cash registers
Play money
Flannel board set
Lacing and zipper boards
Bead Stair
Rig-a-Jig
Playskool Village
Shapes Sorting Box
Pickup sticks
Strings and beads
Stacking toys
Bristle Blocks

Etch-a-Sketch
Snap N' Play School Pack
Play Rings
Fit-a-Square and Circle
Fit-a-Size and Space
Color cube design set
Magic slate
Mosaic
Scope
Lacing boots
Play Tiles
Color Stacking Discs
Toy Maker
Design blocks
Toy hammer-and-nail set

Manipulative-Mathematics Center

Magnet and/or flannel board
Felt primary cutouts
Geometric solids
Plastic counters
Wooden pegs

Dominoes
Rods and Counters
Pegs and pegboard
Playskool Color Cubes
Designs for pegs

Giant counting rods
Color and Shape Bingo
Grouping circles
Arithme-Sticks
Magnetic counting shapes
Counting frame
Colored Cubes
Counters
Colored sticks

Clock face
Play Chips
First Arithmetic Game
Magnetic numbers
Beads and Rods
Attribute blocks
Numberite
Cash register

Homemaking Center

1 stove
1 sink
1 doll bed
1 rocker
2 telephones
1 corn broom
Aluminum pots
1 doll
Mirror
1 ironing board

1 refrigerator
1 cupboard
1 dresser
1 highchair
1 push broom
Aluminum cutlery
Tea set — metal preferred
Plastic fruit and vegetables
1 dustpan
1 iron

Art Center

1 dozen aprons, ages 4-7 size:
  Jericho, Inc., P.O. Box 6591,
  Houston, TX 77005.
12 scissors, right- and left-handed,
  pointed
1 scissor rack
10 sets Payons
10 sets watercolors
10 sets Cray-pas
2 boxes colored chalk
Clay
25 boxes jumbo crayons, no roll
12 boxes small-size crayons
1 dozen ½" paint brushes, flat-end
1 dozen watercolor brushes
2 paper punches

Tempera paint, all colors, liquid
8 jars finger paint
Paste
Glue
6 sponges
6 brayers
1 dozen felt-tip pens
6 tubes water-base printing ink, 2
  black, 2 blue, 2 white
Newsprint easel paper, 18 × 24"
Manila paper, 12 × 18" and 9 × 12"
Construction paper, assorted colors,
  12 × 18" and 9 × 12"
Butcher paper

Woodworking Center

Workbench and vise

1 hand drill

2 saws, 16"

1 brace and bit

Nails, 1-2", large-head

2 C-clamps

Bits for hand drill

2 hammers

Assorted wheels

Sandpaper

Science Center

Animal cages

Aquarium

Magnifying glasses

Prisms

Assorted magnets

Pulley system

Balance scales

Scales (other than balance)

Hot plate

Oven, if possible

Boxed Games

Lotto games

Hickety Pickety

Candyland

Chutes and Ladders

Color and Shapes Bingo

Hi Ho Cherry Oh!

Winnie the Pooh Game

Alphabet or Number Bingo

5.
Art

FIVE important processes form the basis of an art program for young children: drawing, painting, cutting and pasting, modeling, and printing. From these a wide variety of art experiences will emanate. Crayons and easel painting are everyday choices, even when other art activities are available at the art table. Other art activities can be offered once during the year and others only occasionally. A papier-mâché class project could fit the former category and straw painting the latter. The bulk of the art projects will be related to one of the five basic processes.

Successful Art Experiences

If you keep in mind the following tips, any art experience you provide will be a rewarding one for the children.

1. Introduce each new art activity so that the many possibilities offered by any art medium are fully explored and economical use of materials encouraged.
2. At the beginning of the year, take time to talk about materials with which the children are supposed to be acquainted. This discussion is important since materials such as crayons and tempera paint will be used very often in the classroom.
3. Choose materials related to the needs, interests, and capabilities of the children in your class.
4. Offer less complicated projects at the beginning of the year. Later in the year, introduce projects which will take several days to complete.
5. Reinforce the production of art by sharing the children's art work often. Although there will be more sharing in the first few months, this practice needs to be continued all year.
6. Play fair with the children. If you choose to share easel paintings at a meeting time, show all the paintings, not just a few. If art work is not to be shared in front of the group on a particular morning, you can still give recognition to the children who worked at the easel or at the art table. The class can take a few minutes before going outside or after rest to look at art work hung on a clothesline across the room or displayed on a tabletop.

7. Be careful what you say about art work as you are showing it. Teachers are often unaware that value judgments are being made by themselves and the children when they make such comments as, "My, what a beautiful painting," or, "John draws animals so well." It would be more fair to make comments related to the colors used or to the brightness of a color.

8. Do not assume that you can name the subject matter in any piece of art work. A safer approach is to say, "Tell us about your painting," or to ask, "What is happening over here?" or, "Am I holding your painting correctly?"

9. Treat art not as an isolated experience, but rather as an integral part of your total program. The children's art will reflect not only their past experiences, but also what is going on in the classroom. Study-time topics offer a source for many rich ideas for paintings, drawings, modeling, or building experiences. Also, study-time topics can be chosen from the world of art. Interesting studies can be based on Weaving, Pottery, Printmaking, Book Illustration, Children in Art, Masks, Eskimo Art, Art of the Cave Dwellers, or an Artist.

10. Enhance the art experience and promote language development by offering to write the children's words on their art work. If a child is reluctant to have words on the same side as the art work, write the words on the back or on a separate piece of paper. Read the words when the art work is being shared.

11. Bring resource people to the classroom whose interests or talents are related to art. Visit an artist's studio or an art class in process at a high school or college.

12. Offer art books on the library table.

13. Show films related to art.

14. Know your children. Some children will come to the art table with a preconceived negative appraisal of their ability to do art work. Your responsibility is to help every child succeed at the level of his or her capabilities. If a child cannot cut, you can help him or her learn to cut by offering encouragement and by providing opportunities for lots of practice. If the child seems to lack the imagination to think up art subjects, the rich experiences you provide in the classroom will act as a springboard for ideas. Other children in the room will act as catalysts in moving an unproductive child into becoming an active participant at the art table or easel. However, you cannot magically make all your children ready for every experience which they will encounter at the art table. There is a point at which you have the responsibility to make a child aware of his or her limitations at a particular moment in time. This is not a negative appraisal of the child's abilities, but rather a realistic statement of fact. Children are aware of individual differences among them. The class quickly decides on who "draws the goodest."

It is possible to develop an art program in which every child in your classroom can enjoy being at the art table and in which every child will feel comfortable with the art he or she produces, yet be open to improvement and growth.

The Easel

Hold a meeting during the second or third morning to introduce the use of the easel. Bring the easel to a spot in the room where all children can see it. Spread newspapers under it. Demonstrate how to put on an apron or some other kind of covering garment. Pick up a brush loaded with paint and start to paint. Let the children see how the paint drips on the paper and the floor. Ask someone to tell you if that was a good beginning. Ask, "Why not?" and, "What should I have done first?" Demonstrate wiping the brush on both sides before lifting it out of the paint container. Show the array of colors you have on the easel. Take a brush from a dark color, use it, and then return it to a light-color paint container. Show this second container of paint to the children and ask what happened. Ask what could be done if you do make a mistake and put the brush in the wrong container. Tell the children that colors will not be mixed but will be kept separate for now, but that they will have opportunities later to experiment with mixing colors.

Take a brush and ask children to comment on how many ways the paint could be applied with the brush. Responses will probably include making thin or thick lines, dabbing, or laying the brush down flat on the paper.

Use of the Easel

1. The most common materials used at the easel are tempera paint and 18 x 24" newsprint.
2. Occasionally substitute colored butcher paper, newspaper, textured papers, construction paper, finger-paint paper, or paper from a sample book of wallpapers.
3. Use other materials besides tempera paint at the easel, such as: Cray-pas, crayons, Payons, colored chalk, or printing materials.
4. Offer different-size paint brushes, or substitute sticks, shoe-polish dabbers, cotton-tipped sticks for brushes, or roll-on deodorant bottles.
5. Mix up exciting new colors from your stock of paint. Green and yellow, for example, make a lovely spring green.
6. Have the children cover the entire paper with a dark color, let it dry, and then paint with light, bright colors on top of it; or reverse the procedure and let the children cover the paper with a layer of light-colored paint, let it dry, and then paint a picture using black, purple, or red.
7. Add white tempera paint to every color at the easel.
8. Use only one family of colors at the easel.
9. Offer only the three primary colors—red, yellow, and blue. Allow the children to experiment with these colors on the paper. Include an extra container of water in which the children can wash their brushes.
10. Put out paint of only one color and offer colored butcher paper as a painting surface.
11. Coordinate the colors offered at the easel with the colors used on the bulletin boards, or offer colors in keeping with the seasons or special days or holidays.

Crayons

Hold a meeting on the very first day to talk about the different ways that crayons may be used. The children will offer such suggestions as pressing lightly or hard, using the point to dab the surface, using the side of the crayon, or covering the entire surface of the paper with a light color and then making a picture on top of it with darker colors. Ask, also, what kinds of things can be drawn. The children will offer ideas such as houses, themselves, flowers, birds, their dogs, trucks and cars, boats, and airplanes. Summarize their ideas by saying, "You told me that you can draw people, animals, and things from the world around you." Then add, "We will be studying lots of interesting things in the room which will give you many ideas for your art work."

One of the first requests that you can make of your children is for them to draw crayon pictures of themselves. Ask them to draw a picture of just their face on one side of the paper and their full figure on the other side. After sharing the pictures, file them in the children's folders, so that they can be shared at parent conferences and can also be used as a comparison to pictures resulting from a similar teacher request in the spring.

Use of Crayons

1. At the beginning of the year, offer thick crayons to use on either thin white paper or on construction paper. Newsprint used at the easel can also be cut into smaller pieces to be used at the art table or on the floor.
2. Offer thin crayons and additional colors several months after school starts.
3. Use textured papers, such as oatmeal paper.
4. Use sides of broken crayons for rubbings. Place leaves, pennies, paper clips, combs, or shapes cut from sandpaper under thin white paper. Show the children how to keep the objects from moving.
5. Melt down bits and pieces of crayons and remold them into rectangular shapes. The new sticks can be of one color or be multicolored.
6. Use crayons to make a crayon resist. Have the child press very heavily on the crayon while drawing, and then cover the crayoned surface with a very thin tempera-paint wash. Be sure to test your wash before putting it on the art table. If you make it too thick or dark, the crayon drawings will be completely covered.
7. Fold a 9 × 12" piece of light-colored construction paper in half. Open the paper. On half of the inside area, have the children spread a layer of white chalk, then cover it with either crayon of one color, or with stripes or rectangles of many colors. Make sure the crayon layer is waxy. Since some crayons are waxier than others, it might be well for you to experiment first before setting these materials out. Choose colors such as red, black, green, blue, orange, or purple. Remind the children to hold their fingers down near the point of the crayon as they work. When a good layer of wax has been applied over the chalk, have the children close the booklet and make a drawing on the front part by pressing heavily with a primary pencil.

The pressure will lift the crayon wax from the inside and deposit it in reverse on the other half of the inside sheet. Have the children print their names on the outside and discover that they will appear in reverse on the inside. For those children who want their name to "look right," have them print their name on a separate piece of paper and give them a small hand mirror to hold up near their name to see how they will have to print it to have it appear correctly on the inside.

Other Art Experiences

Cray-pas. Cray-pas can be purchased at stores which sell art supplies. (The name *Cray-pas* is a combination of parts of the words *crayon* and *pastel*.) They are available singly or in various-size boxes. Cray-pas are similar to oil pastels. They do not have as long a life span as crayons and the cost is higher. Nevertheless, each year I purchase a new supply, and as they break up into small pieces I add them to a basket of pieces accumulated from previous years. Children respond to the brilliant colors available and to the waxy texture of Cray-pas on paper. Beautiful Cray-pas-resist pictures can be made by covering a completed Cray-pas picture with a very thin tempera paint wash.

When Cray-pas are introduced to the children, let them know that you are aware that they will break very easily and that it doesn't matter. The children can be reminded, however, to hold their fingers close to the point of the Cray-pas as they work.

Payons. Payons resemble crayons except that they usually have a heavy paper covering on them. (Payons can be ordered from Practical Drawing Co., P.O. Box 5388, Dallas, TX 75222.) Payons can be used like crayons. However, if a watercolor effect is wanted, have the children use a wet watercolor brush on the colored areas after the picture is drawn. Be sure the children wash their brushes as they use them to wet different colored areas. For an instant watercolor effect, Payons can also be dipped in water as the picture is being made.

Watercolors. Watercolor paints are available in sets of colors or in individual cakes. Plastic containers for sets of watercolor paint eliminate the rust problem and make cleanup easier.

Watercoloring is another activity which needs to be introduced to the children early in the year. Most children respond very positively to this experience, perhaps because of the liquid quality of the paint or the fact that children do not seem to feel that they must make a representational drawing with watercolor paints. There seems to be less concern about the product.

Prepare the art table before the meeting by placing a set of watercolors and paper for each child and a jar of water for every two children. Use jars which are low, wide-mouthed, and have enough weight to keep them upright on the table. Ask the children how the paint can be picked up on the watercolor brush. Demonstrate dipping the brush into the water, retaining the water by not wiping the brush, rolling only the bristle part of the brush onto the cake of paint, then applying it to the paper. Ask the children what should be done next if another color is going to be used.

Several weeks later, show the children how to wet the entire surface of the paper with a two-inch brush before applying any color to the paper. Let the children see how the colors run together, making new colors. Be sure to leave an extra jar of clean water in the middle of the table to be used only for wetting the clean paper.

Another variation of this same activity is to introduce the use of water-color pans or pallettes. Show the children how to pick up a small amount of water and deposit it in one of the depressions in the pan. Then demonstrate picking up colors to be mixed.

Colored Chalk. Chalk can be used on a dry surface and sprayed with hair spray, which acts as a fixative; or on a surface which has been dampened with a wet sponge. Chalk can also be dipped in water or buttermilk as the picture is being made. Ask the children questions concerning how the chalk can be held to produce different effects. This same procedure was suggested for crayons on page 52.

Cut-and-Paste Activities. You can offer a variety of experiences with the same materials.

1. Offer precut multicolored shapes. Ask questions to get some ideas about what could be made with the shapes.
2. Put out a box of small scraps for the children to cut and paste. Let the children make what they want.
3. Offer scraps of construction paper with pleasing color combinations. Examples: black, turquoise, and pink; or hot colors—yellow, red, and orange.
4. Make available paper from one family of colors. Examples: pink, red, red-purple, and purple.
5. Suggest the subject matter: "Today our art project will be to make a make-believe animal." Or, "Today our pictures will be about hamsters." Or, "Today we will be making designs."
6. Offer a box of multicolored two-inch squares of paper. Talk about patterns. Look at cloth samples of repeated patterns. Also show a checkerboard as an example of a pattern. Let the children "read" the pattern.
7. Have the children draw outline pictures of people and animals and decorate them by using small scraps of paper for body coverings or clothing.

Tear Pictures. Set out scraps of construction paper for tearing. Hold a meeting and ask the children how you can get desired shapes without using scissors. Demonstrate how to tear slowly and how to build up a picture layer by layer.

Finger Paint. Set out finger-paint paper or glossy shelf paper, one jar of finger paint, a tablespoon, and water in a plastic dispenser such as is used to sprinkle clothes before ironing. Remind the children about covering garments or aprons before they start. Show the children how to sprinkle their paper with water to get a slick surface and then how to put a tablespoon of finger paint on it. Then ask them how the finger paint could be distributed over the surface. The children will suggest using the palms of the hands, the side of the hand, tips of the fingers, and the like. Accept all of these suggestions.

If you are offering finger paint as the art activity, stay in the vicinity of the art table while the painting is going on. You will need to handle wet paintings as they are completed. If they are not dripping, paintings can be hung on the clothesline or placed on a standing clothes dryer. Newspapers can be spread out on the floor for the wettest pictures. If the children are not able to glide their hands smoothly over the paper's surface, remind them to sprinkle a little more water on it and to add another spoonful of paint.

On another occasion, offer two primary colors at the art table, so that the children can discover what happens when certain colors are mixed. Offer red and yellow, blue and yellow, or red and blue.

After using finger paint a few times, ask the children what kind of things they could paint with finger paint. If older children in the building have been using finger paint, their paintings might be shared with the younger children to generate new ideas.

Collage and Glue Activities. Children greatly enjoy being able to rummage around in a tray or box of assorted materials for things to glue onto a surface. The tray could hold buttons, pretend gems from old dime-store jewelry, pieces of cloth of various textures (satin, velvet, silk), feathers, cotton balls, different kinds of paper (tissue, cellophane, wrapping), ribbons, used greeting cards, pieces from games no longer used, collections of various kinds of seeds, macaroni, or colored toothpicks. The children can use small individual bottles of glue or glue placed in a styrofoam cup inside a flat-bottomed jar. Be sure to wash the lids or caps of glue bottles and brushes each time glue is used.

Printing Projects

Many different kinds of materials can be used for successful printing experiences.

Potato Prints

Potato prints can be made by the children quite easily if you hold a short meeting to introduce some of the necessary steps. Before the children arrive at school, prepare four potatoes by cutting them in half; make sure that each cut surface is flat. Cut designs into the surface, as illustrated in the following diagram. Place some tempera paint on the art table. Call a meeting and ask the children to describe the materials that are on the art table. Also ask what they think will be done at the art table that morning. Demonstrate how to pick up paint, wipe the brush, and apply the paint smoothly to the surface of the potato. Ask the children why paint is not being applied to the cutout areas. With the paper flat on the table, show the children how to place the potato carefully on the paper, apply pressure to it without wiggling it, and lift it off the paper. Ask what they think might happen if you moved the painted potato on the paper. You might demonstrate the result. Then ask

Potato Prints

Cut away darkened areas.

how a second print may be made with the same potato. Remind the children that once they use a color on a piece of potato, they should continue using the same color.

A variation of this activity is to ask the children at a meeting what would happen if many prints were made from the potato after one application of paint. Demonstrate the result. Ask what happened. You might also talk about overprinting and discuss colors which, when placed on top of each other, will produce a new color. Set out yellow and blue in one area and red and yellow in another for experimentation. Potato prints can be used to decorate wrapping paper, paper tablecloths for parties, or covers of books made by the children.

Vegetable and Fruit Prints

Oranges and lemons make good prints. Ask the children what will happen if they press the fruit too hard while making their prints.

Carrots and onions can be used. Onions offer an interesting pattern but have a tendency to fall apart from use. Turnips or rutabagas would be appropriate also, though a little harder to cut.

Art Gum Eraser Prints

These erasers can be cut with a razor blade or exacto knife. Buy the longer variety, as the children can grasp them more easily.

Clay Prints

Pull out a handle from a three-inch ball of clay. Mash one end of the clay on a flat surface and then make a design on this area by making indentations with a nail head, the end of a Tinker Toy stick, or some other cylindrically shaped object. The prints are more successful when the clay is still somewhat soft. Have the children paint the designed area with tempera paint and ask them not to apply too much pressure as they make their prints on paper.

Cardboard Prints

Have the children cut up pieces of thin cardboard (shirt cardboard, for example) and build up designs by pasting cut pieces on thicker pieces of cardboard no larger than 6 × 8″. After a three-dimensional effect has been obtained, have the children roll on tempera paint. For this activity, place slightly thick tempera paint in a tray with low sides and have the children use a brayer to pick up the paint to be rolled on the cardboard surface. Demonstrate how to lay a sheet of white paper carefully on top of the cardboard, to press carefully with the palm of their hand, and to pick up the paper starting at one corner and peeling it off.

Woodblock or Linoleum Prints

Prints can be made from woodblocks and linoleum blocks if you prepare these surfaces or have an artist cut designs in them. A few children probably could be taught how to use woodcutting tools, but the tools would be dangerous in the hands of most young children. I would suggest using a water-base printing ink, even though prints made from these inks do have a longer drying time than prints made with oil-base inks. These water-base printing inks can be purchased at art-supply stores. The price is fairly reasonable since a tube of ink will last quite a long time.

At a meeting, have brayers or rollers available and a surface on which the ink can be rolled. I use small pieces of linoleum. After the ink is picked up on the roller, demonstrate how to roll it smoothly one way onto the surface of the block. Place the paper carefully on the block, centering it as best as you can, and move the palm smoothly back and forth, applying pressure at the same time. Special tools called barens can be purchased for this process if desired. Once again lift the paper at one corner and peel it off the block.

Sponge Prints

Cut up four sponges into various shapes—squares, rectangles, triangles. Wet the sponges and squeeze out the excess water. Place them on the art table along with a muffin pan holding different-colored tempera paint. Place on the table folded paper towels to be used as blotters for excess paint. Clothespins can be attached to the pieces of sponge for easier holding and dipping. Offer newsprint paper 18 × 24″ or construction paper 12 × 18″. When the meeting is called, ask the children what they think will be done at the art table that morning. Demonstrate dipping the sponge into the paint and placing it first on the folded paper towel and then on the paper. Talk about the kind of texture that is produced and why the empty spaces are visible.

Ask the children why the blotter is used first and what would happen if you pressed the sponge down very hard on the paper. Demonstrate the results of picking up too much paint, not blotting, and applying too much pressure on the sponge. Sponge prints can be used to decorate paper tablecloths for parties or tissue paper used for wrapping clay products or other gifts.

Kitchen-Gadget Prints

Let the children experiment with different kitchen equipment to see what kind of prints they can make. The consistency of the tempera paint needs to be thicker than for other printing procedures. Examples: fork, a potato masher, cork, cake server, or spatula.

Monoprints

Let the children prepare their finger paintings on pieces of linoleum and then show them how to place a piece of paper over the finger-paint surface, press down carefully over the entire surface with the palm of the hand, then pick up their paper from one corner and peel it off the linoleum. After the print has been made, ask the children if they will be able to make a second identical print from the same surface. Write the word *monoprint* on a piece of paper and talk about the meaning of *mono*. Introduce the words *monologue* and *monocle*.

Tissue-Paper Pictures

Set out multicolored tissue paper which has been cut into small pieces, 4 × 4" or so. Place liquid starch in low, wide-mouthed jars—one container for every two children. Have available 1-2" paint brushes. Ask the children to describe the materials on the art table. It is possible that no one will recognize the starch. You might remind them about how daddy's shirts come back from the laundry with stiff collars or how little girls' dresses used to be starched. Ask them if they see any glue on the table and then, what might be used in its place. Lay several colored pieces of tissue paper flat on a piece of construction paper and brush a layer of liquid starch over it. The children will be able to comment on the holding power of the starch.

Stencils

Make several stencils of different sizes out of illustration board. Include the various shapes—circles, ovals, triangles, squares, and rectangles. Place thin crayons on the art table. Show the stencils to the children and ask how they think they could be used at the art table. The children will probably be able to describe the procedure. Show a cardboard square and ask the children how to transfer the shape of the cardboard square to a piece of paper. The children will suggest drawing around the square. Then ask if this activity is the same as using a stencil.

On other occasions offer stencils relating to a holiday, such as cutout hearts for Valentine's Day, bats and witches for Halloween, or Christmas trees for Christmas and menorahs or dreidels for Chanukah.

Stencil

Place stencil over paper.
Color in.
Remove stencil.

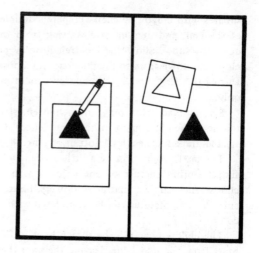

Let the children cut stencils of their own from shirt cardboard if they are able to, or from squares of construction paper. Demonstrate how to fold the paper so that only one half of the shape need be cut.

Caution: Use these kind of stencils sparingly. They are *no* substitute for children creating their own art.

Simple Sewing Projects

Take time to discuss how to use needles safely, how to knot the thread, and how to make a plain running stitch. For the first experience, have ready six-inch squares of burlap, multicolored embroidery thread, and embroidery needles and chalk. It might be necessary for you to stitch around the outside edges of the burlap to keep it from unravelling. Make several lines on the

Sewing Stitches

Outline leaves with running stitch.
Work stem in running stitch.

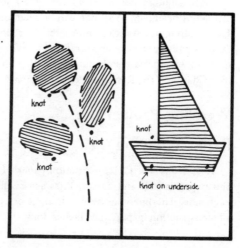

squares with crayon or chalk. Prepare a double strand of thread, make a knot at the end, and demonstrate starting from the wrong side so that the knot does not show. Show the children how to push the needle up through the cloth and down again to the underside, and how to pull all the thread through. During this first session the children should practice making lines of stitches only.

Set up places for only four children, since the activity will take more teacher time than many other experiences. Children will need help getting started, threading needles, knotting the thread, and ending off rows of stitches.

The next project can be a little more involved. Ask the children to draw a simple outline picture of one object on the square of cloth. Children will choose such subject matter as flowers, houses, trees, boats, hearts, faces, or animals. The pictures can be completed with embroidery threads of different colors.

The children can also be shown how to fill in an area with a long stitch. Start from the underside, leaving the knot there, come up on one edge of the design, make a long stitch to the other side of the design, pull the needle through to the underside, and come up again on the edge of the design where you started. Repeat, filling in the whole area.

Bean Bags

For this project have ready samples of five-inch squares of cloth pinned together in twos. Ask the children what they will have to think about when they stitch the two pieces of cloth together. (Answers: No big holes can be left or the beans will fall out. A place has to be left open for putting the beans inside.) Use regular needles and strong thread for this project. The children will probably have to go around the sides twice, leaving open a small area on one side. Check their stitches before allowing the children to fill their bean bags. I suggest that you close up the openings.

Some children will want to turn their joined pieces of cloth into purses instead of bean bags. A ribbon can be sewn onto the sides for a simple handle. The children may want to embroider their cloth before stitching it together.

This activity can be encouraged by inviting resource people into the classroom to demonstrate embroidery, needlepoint, crewel, crocheting, or knitting. (See Chapter VIII, Resource People.)

Weaving Projects

Paper Weaving

Have ready 9 × 12″ construction paper which has been prepared by folding the paper in half and cutting lines across the paper to about one inch from each side. The lines can be cut straight or curved. Precut multicolored strips of construction paper nine inches long. It might be well to show a woven

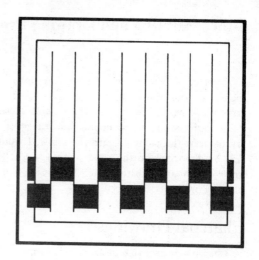

placemat or some other objects on which the weaving can be seen very plainly, and then demonstrate weaving the paper in and out of the cut lines. Although this activity may seem very simple to an adult, it is not easy for most children. You will need a great deal of patience in helping children understand what they need to do to weave successfully. I would suggest that only a few children work at the art table at one time so that you will be able to give attention to the children needing help.

Cardboard Weaving

Prepare simple looms by cutting slits into two opposite sides of cardboard pieces about six inches square. Use cotton rug yarn or thick wool yarn. Have the children use some precut lengths of yarn as a pattern for cutting enough yarn for the vertical and horizontal threads. The children then fasten the vertical yarns through the slits, leaving a small piece of yarn dangling. The children either weave the yarn in and out of the vertical threads by using their fingers, or with the aid of a small piece of cardboard or wood with a slit for fastening the yarn.

Bring all dangling leftover yarn to the underside and at the completion of the project fasten these loose threads on the underside with a piece of masking tape.

Pot Holders

Simple metal looms are available with which children can use cotton loops to make a woven pot holder. Most kindergarten-age children can complete this project by the spring of the year.

Other Painting and Drawing Projects

Straw Printing

Children are quite excited about the novelty of using straws to paint, but many find that they get rather tired during the process. Purchase wide plastic straws and use fairly thin tempera paint so that the children can blow the paint more easily. Since many children get a mouthful of paint when they try to draw the paint up into the straw, I would suggest that drops of paint first be deposited on the paper with a brush. Then show the children how to kneel down and position their straws very close to the paint drop before blowing on it.

Charcoal Drawings

Charcoal is available at art-supply stores in various shapes and sizes. At a short meeting to introduce this activity, ask questions about how to hold the charcoal to get different kinds of lines and how to get variations in color.

Pencil Drawings

Set out pencils of various hardnesses and paper of different textures for the children to try. You might hold a question-and-answer period before or after the work is completed.

Brayer Painting

Trays with low sides can hold the tempera paint. You will need to experiment yourself first to see what results can be obtained with various paint consistencies. Brayers or rollers are available at art-supply stores, the same brayers as are used in printmaking. They are rather inexpensive. Set out construction paper that is 12 × 18" in size. The idea is not to cover the paper surface with a smooth layer of paint, but to get some interesting textures and mixing of colors as one color is rolled over another.

Drawing with India Ink and Water-Soluble Inks

This activity is enjoyed by children but is not offered too often because of the high cost of the inks. For pens, I have used small sticks found on the playground or pen staffs with artist's pen nibs. At a meeting held to talk about the materials, questions will need to be asked about the proper and safe way to use the pens. Set the ink bottles inside another jar before the children begin.

White ink on black paper or black ink on white paper produces interesting pictures.

Three-Dimensional Animals

When this project is introduced, there is usually very good response on the part of the children. Since it does take a lot of teacher time, it will be necessary to tell the children that all children who want to make an animal will have the opportunity to do so, but that it may be some days before they can get started.

Have ready butcher paper that has been cut into rectangles about 20 × 24" in size. Ask the children for ideas as to what kinds of animals could be made. Describe the process of making a simple outline drawing on one sheet of paper, cutting it out, and using it as a pattern for the second sheet. After making sure that the two sides of the cutout match each other, demonstrate the use of a stapler to staple the two sheets of paper together, leaving an opening large enough so that the children can stuff crumpled pieces of newspapers through it. After the animal has been filled, close the opening with staples.

Ask the children for ideas for decorating the animals. Some children may prefer to use crayons on the two sheets before they are stapled together, while others may want to use tempera paint after the animal has been stuffed. *Note:* Be sure to check the drawings before the children start to cut. Many times they will include drawings of parts which will necessitate intricate cutting and make joining and stuffing difficult. At the initial meeting, it might be a good idea to discuss this problem before it occurs. Talk about making all the parts wide enough to be stapled and stuffed.

Clay

A few materials are absolutely necessary to have available for young children to use. Clay falls in this category. In my judgment, play dough and plasticine are not satisfactory substitutes. The clay should be prewedged and soft enough to be used by young children. If a kiln is available, the clay can be bisque fired, glazed, and then refired.

For a first experience, have the art table set up with pieces of linoleum or smooth wood on which individual children will be working. Clay tools can be introduced the second time that clay is made available. Have the large box-shaped pieces of clay on the table for the children to see. Ask what they know about it. Some children will call it play dough. Give it its proper name. Cut a piece of clay off and ask how the shape can be changed. For the first experience, it is important that the children have an opportunity to experience the feel of the clay and to find out how they can use their hands or fingers as tools to shape and reshape the clay. In any kindergarten room, there will be children who will influence inexperienced children by forming an ashtray or some other object. Accept these products and ask what other kinds of shapes can be modeled from the clay.

Let the children put their clay constructions on a tray to dry. Be sure to mark their names or initials on the bottom with a nail or toothpick; very often children will forget which is theirs after two or three days. If the children want to paint the dried clay pieces, set up different colors of tempera paint on the art table. Some children will want to leave the clay in its natural color. Since tempera paint will rub off, you can apply a thin coat of clear lacquer over the painted surfaces before the children take them home. It might be worthwhile for you to take time to wrap the clay products in a few layers of newspaper, with the children's names clearly written on the outside. It will save many a child's tears and hurt feelings over broken clay objects.

After the children have had a few chances to experiment with clay, hold another meeting to talk about things that can be made out of clay. It would be very appropriate to present this activity along with a unit or some learning sequences on clay. A unit can be planned in several different ways; for instance, "How have humans used clay throughout history?" or the teaching can be subsumed under a larger unit on Mexico. Many rich experiences can be presented to the children to broaden their concept of clay and of products made from clay, and to enhance their own ideas about clay constructions. An objective might be that children would begin to appreciate the aesthetic as well as the utilitarian aspect of clay products.

If you present a study on clay, you might include a visit to a potter's studio or to a ceramics class in progress at a high school or college so children can see students at work. If there is an art teacher at your school, she or he might have access to a potter's wheel to demonstrate throwing a pot, or else show how pots and figures can be formed without the use of a potter's wheel. Films are also available which demonstrate this art form.

As I write about these experiences for children, I know that some teachers will disagree with my ideas about showing finished products to young children. I appreciate their concern that young children will feel inadequate about their clay constructions. In the introductory section to this chapter I expressed the need for children to face the reality of their limitations at some time. Most young children are quite aware of differences that exist between their art and the art produced by older children or young adults. They are astutely aware of differences that exist in their own classroom within their peer group. However, this awareness does not impede children from participating at the art table nor does it unduly influence their art work. What can interfere is a teacher who does not know how to provide a program in which all children will feel good about the art they produce.

Clay Tools

At another meeting about clay, ask the children to name the best tools they have to work with clay. (Answer: their hands.) Introduce some other clay tools. If you cannot purchase these metal and wooden tools, substitute Popsicle sticks; some kitchen gadgets like pastry cutters, metal spatulas, and melon cutters; nails; and screws. Ask how these items might be used. Let the children once again experiment with the clay.

Clay Containers

During the next discussion about clay, introduce the idea of making containers. Show some examples of clay containers and demonstrate how they can be made by various methods if they do not already know them. If a film on clay has been shown, the children will be able to offer many ideas. The pinch, coil, or slab method of building can be introduced. Be sure to talk about adequate thickness of parts. The children can decorate the sides of their containers by using some of the clay tools.

Clay Animals

With just a few introductory questions, children can be helped to make their own models of real or make-believe animals independently. Have ready good-size balls of clay—as big as your fist. Ask the children how they can form a head without adding another piece of clay onto the ball. Someone will offer the suggestion to pinch or pull a portion out. Demonstrate this method and pull a portion of clay out until it is held by a very thin strand of clay, so that the head bends or breaks off. Ask the children what was the matter with the way you did it. Children will understand that when a portion of the clay is pulled out, the connecting strand must be thick enough to hold the weight of the newly formed part. Make the ball of clay whole again and this time pull out a head leaving the connecting part thicker than before. Ask the children how legs or a tail can be formed. Demonstrate pulling out the various parts. Ask how the animal you have made could be made more interesting. Once the meeting is over, re-form your clay animal into a ball.

If children want to join parts onto the ball, it might be good to talk about this process with the whole class. The new parts will adhere to the larger portion if the ends of the added part and the place where it will be attached are made rough with a nail or some other tool. Slightly wet the areas to be joined and run your fingers over the joint, bringing clay from the larger part over the added part.

In most schools it will not be possible to fire all of the children's clay products. Many schools do not have a kiln. If this is the case, perhaps arrangements could be made to have a potter fire the children's work at least several times through the year. Once the clay is bisque fired, the children can glaze their objects in the classroom and then the clay can be fired a second time.

Life-Size Self-Portraits

Since this project will take a lot of teacher time, it will be necessary to introduce the project and then have it continue until all children who want to make a portrait have done so. You will need precut colored butcher paper as long as the tallest child in the room. An alternate art activity will need to be offered at the art table while the self-portraits are being completed.

Ask "How can you make a full-size drawing of yourself?" Someone will suggest laying a child on a piece of paper and drawing around him or her. Demonstrate by using one of the children. Ask what should be done next. After cutting out the shape of the child, ask how this shape can be made to resemble the child more accurately. Children will suggest adding and coloring hair, making the eyes, nose, and mouth, and perhaps decorating the shape with clothing similar to that which the model is wearing.

When the work begins, some children will have difficulty with the cutting process. You have the choice either to help these children yourself or ask children who can cut to aid other children.

After the figures are completed, display them on a hallway wall and put the children's names beside them.

Papier-Mâché Projects

If you want to have the children work on individual projects, I would suggest you keep them rather small. Most young children do not seem to be motivated enough to work the necessary number of days to complete a large papier-mâché project. Children can make individual Easter eggs by molding paper strips with wheat paste on them over a partially blown-up oval-shaped balloon, or they can fashion a small maraca by wrapping the paper strips over a small burned-out light bulb. After the bulb has a thick covering of paper strips, tap the bulb on the floor to break the glass so that the maraca will make sounds when shaken. When completely dry, the Easter eggs or maraca can be painted with tempera paint. You can seal the painted surface with a coat of clear lacquer. Be sure to keep a window open as you work with lacquer and have the work area well protected with newspapers.

Many children are willing to work on a class project in papier-mâché. A little work can be done each morning for a number of days until the project is completed. Making a piñata during a study on Mexico might be enough motivation to provide you with lots of willing workers.

Two-Dimensional Paper Marionettes

Cut construction paper into large rectangles (6 X 9") for bodies, smaller rectangles (4 X 6") to be cut into heads and necks, and narrow rectangles (2 X 6") which will be used for arms or legs. Place brads in a dish on the art table. Tell the children the project on the art table will be to make marionettes with arms, legs, and heads that move. Ask how the parts might be joined. Let a child demonstrate how to use a brad to hold the parts together. Ask why the parts weren't stapled or glued together. Discuss how the marionettes could be decorated once the parts are all joined together. A string can be attached at the top of the head for the child to hold. Use a paper punch to make the holes.

6.
Music

I N most kindergarten classrooms, the teacher is responsible for teaching all areas of the curriculum, including music. Many teachers of young children express some discomfort or feelings of inadequacy in this area. These feelings could in part be attributed to a lack of formal training in music and a belief that it is necessary to have musical talent in order to provide musical experiences for young children.

Before going further, I would like to reassure beginning teachers that it is possible to provide adequate, even rich, musical experiences without having musical talent or formal training in music. Two prerequisites will balance the scale for the teacher—a love of music and a belief that music is important enough to be a part of every school day.

Basic to every music program is the singing of songs. Sing with the children every day—not just at times designated "Music Time," but at any opportune moment. Sing to greet the new day, sing directions and messages. At first the children will be startled by your behavior, but in a day or so their surprise will turn to joy. They'll soon accept it as very natural behavior, something that fits into, and is an integral part of, the school day.

Sing nursery rhymes, songs that the children already know, finger plays, fill-in songs, musical games, cowboy songs, patriotic songs, popular songs, and folk songs from our country and from foreign countries.

I feel that the songs most appropriate for young children are folk songs. If asked why, I would offer the following reasons:
- Children love folk songs and respond to them.
- Folk songs tell stories and children love stories.
- A great variety is available. While some folk songs are happy or sad, others are funny or exciting.
- Folk songs are easy to learn.
- Folk songs are worth learning. Since they have been around so long, they must have value. It might be that they reflect universal feelings with which we can all identify.

Before introducing folk songs to the children, it might be good to talk with them about the term "folk song." Write the words on the chalkboard and have a short question-and-answer period to help clarify the meaning of the word "folk." Guide the children as follows:

- How might you tell your mother and father about a song you heard? Would you have to know how to write it down? (You could sing it to them.)
- What if you forgot some of the words? (You could make up some of your own.)
- What if you didn't like some of the words? (You could change them.)
- You know, the things that we have been talking about have actually happened. Most folk songs were handed down by people or by "folk" singing them to other "folk" or people—perhaps it was a mother to her child, a grandfather to his grandchild, or someone to a friend. Sometimes the people forgot the words or changed them. Many folk songs were made up so long ago that no one knows who wrote them. Most of the songs we will be learning at school will be folk songs.

Sources for Folk Songs

Many fine collections of folk songs are available in books or on record or tape. Some books which would enhance your music program would be:

Boni, Margaret Bradford. *Fireside Book of Folk Songs for Children.* Simon and Schuster, 1947.

Engvick, William (ed.). *Night Songs and Lullabies.* Harper, 1965.

Landek, Beatrice. *Songs to Grow On.* Edward B. Marks Music Corp., Wm. Sloan Associates, 1950.

_____ . *More Songs to Grow On.* Edward B. Marks Music Corp., Wm. Sloan Associates, 1950.

Seeger, Ruth Crawford. *American Folk Songs for Children.* Doubleday, 1948. (This is my first choice.)

Teaching a Song

Choose a folk song from one of the books listed in the previous section. *Song:* "Ducks in the Millpond," from Seeger's *American Folk Songs for Children,* p. 122.

Ducks in the millpond, a-geese
    in the clover, a-
Fell in the millpond,
    a-wet all over.

Chorus
Lawd, Lawd,
Gonna get on a rinktum
Lawd, Lawd,
Gonna get on a rinktum

Ducks in the millpond, a-geese
  in the clover,
Jumped in the bed,
  and the bed turned over.

Monkey in the barnyard,
  a-monkey in the stable,
Monkey get your haircut,
  as soon as you're able.

Had a little pony, his name
  was Jack,
I put him in the stable, and
  he jumped through a crack.

Ducks in the millpond, a-geese
  in the ocean,
A-hug them pretty girls, if
  I take the notion.

Time needed to teach the song: 10-15 minutes.
Procedure: Before introducing it to the children, learn it yourself. Practice singing it so that you know the tune and words. If you don't play the piano or read music, ask someone who does to play it for you on several different occasions until you have the tune firmly fixed in your head.

Gather the children near you and tell them you are going to sing a folk song to them that you would like them to learn. Sing the first verse while the children listen, then ask them to join you as you sing it again. Tell the children that the song has a special part called the chorus, which is sung after each verse. Sing the chorus and then ask the children to sing it with you. If a child asks what the words mean, you might say that you don't know or that perhaps the words are nonsense words. If you are curious, some research might be in line.

Sing the first verse and the chorus. Sing the second verse through, and then have the children sing it with you the second time. Go back and sing the first two verses, adding the chorus each time. If the children are having difficulty, stop there and introduce the other verses the next day after you review what has already been taught. If the children are able to remember the words of the first two verses, go ahead with the remaining verses. Since the verses are short and humorous, it is often possible to teach the five verses at one sitting. Review the song the next day. Sing the song again the next week.

Note: If a child says as you begin, "I already know that song," say, "I'm so glad you do. You'll be able to help me teach it to the other children who don't know it. Sing it with me."

Song: "The Noble Duke of York," from Landek's *More Songs to Grow On,* p. 106.

Oh, the noble Duke of York.

He had ten thousand men,

He marched them up to the top of the hill

And marched them down again.

And when you're up, you're up,

And when you're down, you're down,

And when you're only half-way up

You are neither up nor down.

Time needed to teach the song: 10-15 minutes.
Procedure:

- First day. Sing the whole song to the children so that they can get the feel of it. Sing the first four lines again and then have the class sing them with you. Sing the first verse together once more. Sing the next four lines alone. Let the children sing it with you. Then sing the whole song together.
- Second day. Sing the song to the children, letting those who know it join in. Sing it once more.

Song-related Activities

- Have the children seated on the floor near you. As the children sing the words "up to the top of the hill," they stand up. When they sing "down again," they sit down. When the words "half-way up" are sung, the children crouch. Then, on the last line, they stand when they sing "up" and sit when they sing "down."
- Divide the class into two groups. As one group sings, the second group acts out the song. Have the children line up across one side of the room. Let one member of the group become the Duke who will lead the march. As the song is sung, the children march across the room (up the hill) and back to their starting point (down the hill). Half-way up would be midpoint between these two locations. Reverse the roles so that the second group of children has a turn to march.

Variations with One Song

Very often teachers do not realize that many enjoyable activities can be derived from one song. This next section will explore some of the ways to enrich your music program by using just one song in many different ways.
Song: "Skip to my Lou," from Landek's *Songs to Grow On*, p. 104.

Verse

Lost my partner, what'll I do,

Lost my partner, what'll I do,

Lost my partner, what'll I do?

Skip to my Lou, my darling.

Chorus

Lou, Lou, Skip to my Lou

Lou, Lou, Skip to my Lou

Lou, Lou, Skip to my Lou

Skip to my Lou, my darling.

- Everybody sings it together.
- Sing it softly; sing it loudly.
- Sing the verses loudly, and the chorus softly; or the reverse.
- One group sings while the other group hums or whistles, if they can.
- Round the mouth and sing the song with the "oooo" sound which results.
- Use kazoos or tissue paper over combs.
- Some children accompany the others with Jew's harps.
- One child plays the autoharp, or the teacher plays it, as the class sings.
- One group sings while the other claps hands or slaps knees.
- One group plays rhythm sticks while the other sings.
- The children play various kinds of rhythm-band instruments such as triangles, sandblocks, bells, tone blocks, or tambourines.
- Move to the music.
- Bounce large balls to the music.
- The teacher (or child) plays ukulele, guitar, drum, or tambourine as the others sing.
- Dance a simple square dance to the song.
- Listen to various folk singers' renditions of the song.
- Make up your own words.

Examples:

Jump, jump, jump to my Lou

Hop, hop, hop to my Lou

Crawl, crawl, crawl to my Lou

Slide, slide, slide to my Lou

Blink, blink, blink to my Lou

Clap, clap, clap your hands

Snap, snap, snap your fingers

- Use different children's names.

Examples:

Bill, Bill, jump up high

Ann, Ann, slide, slide, slide

- Make up nonsense words. One child names an animal and another names a funny place for the animal to be.

Examples:

Cows in the kitchen, moo, moo, moo

Tigers in the bedroom, what'll I do?

Hens in the bathtub, cluck, cluck, cluck

Example of procedure: Gather the children near you. Sing the song together. Ask the following questions:

- What did the words tell you to do? (Skip.)
- Let me write that word on the board: s-k-i-p. (Say the letters as you print them.) Could you think of another word to replace the word *skip* in the song? (Run, hop, crawl, jump.)
- Let me write all of those words on the board. Thank you for all your ideas.

Note: Precisely at this point some beginning teachers have a problem. How do you allow children to move about the room without them getting out of hand, such as bumping into each other and the furniture, knocking things over, or not doing what has been agreed upon? A possible solution is for you to say at this point:

- Now that we have listed some things that we could do to this music, what might be some good things for us to think about before we start to move around the room? Can you think of a few rules which might help us to take care of each other and our room while we are enjoying ourselves?

The children might respond:

- Not bump into each other.
- Not run into the furniture or toys.
- Not all do it at the same time; take turns.
- Do what the words say.
- All go in the same direction, not all over the room any old way.

If the children do not think of these answers, guide their thinking by asking:

- What might happen if we don't watch where we are going?
- Is it all right to do anything we want? Why not?
- Will you have a chance to try out your own ideas sometimes?
- Should some of us go one way and some another? Why not?

After a short discussion, divide the class into two groups. Let one group sing the song while the other group moves to the music. Alternate the groups.

Dealing with Problem Behavior

The Disruptive Child

If, after you have discussed appropriate behaviors, a child disrupts the activity, it is wise to take care of the matter promptly. Sometimes, just a touch on the child's shoulder, a glance, or a whispered message will be sufficient reminder to the child. Occasionally, it will be necessary to remove the child from the moving group. Bring the child to a quiet corner and tell him or her: "I am sorry that you were not able to help us today. You will have another chance to try another day."

The Reluctant Child

If the child shows reluctance early in the year, let the child just watch. Most children will be willing to join in after they have had a chance to watch several different kinds of musical activities. If the behavior persists, it might be good to speak to the child's parents or to a former teacher. I would also suggest recording the child's reactions from other parts of the day and various other kinds of activities to see if a pattern of behavior can be determined. Sometimes the reason for nonparticipation by boys in "dancing" or "moving to music" can be attributed to an attitude that these behaviors are not appropriate for boys. Sometimes older siblings or parents have reinforced this attitude. It is possible to modify the attitude, but it will take time, patience, and some teacher ingenuity to provide interesting musical experiences in which most children will want to participate. A study on dance which includes visits by male ballet or folk dancers to the school can help to overcome the notion that these activities are reserved for girls only.

Terminating an Active Session

It is natural for children to get excited during an active musical experience. This outcome can be disturbing to the new teacher who is not always sure that she or he can settle the children down and guide them into the next activity. Some suggestions which might help are:

- If the children are spread around the room at the end of an activity, ask them to stand still until you come and touch them on the head, which will be their signal to fall in line behind you. Just walk around the room tapping the children and lead them to the location of the next activity.
- As an activity ends, start singing or saying:

I'm so happy clap, clap, clap,

I'm so happy tap, tap, tap,

I'm so happy I turn around,

I'm so happy I sit down.

As you start to sing it a second time, the children will join in. When they have sat down, they can be given their next set of directions.

- As an activity ends, tell the children that they are frozen into statues and only you have the magic touch that will unfreeze them. As you touch each child, whisper where he or she is to go.
- As soon as the activity ends, begin a finger play that the children already know or start to read a picture storybook that you have left in a convenient place. Most children will join in whatever activity you begin. If one or two do not, as you continue saying the verse or reading the story, get up and gather the strays, and, without saying a word, lead them back to the group. Then sit down and go right on with your activity.
- Before beginning the last part of any active period, tell the children where they are to meet you when the activity ends.

Introducing Rhythm Instruments

Most classrooms have some rhythm-band instruments for the children to use. These generally include any of the following:

- triangles
- bells
- sandblocks
- rhythm sticks
- drums
- tone blocks
- clackers
- maracas
- cymbals (finger or regular-size)

For beginning experiences, it might be wise to introduce each instrument separately on different occasions. Introduce rhythm sticks first, probably after the children have learned to sing four or five songs, around the end of the second week of school.

Procedure: Hold a pair of rhythm sticks in your hands and ask the children to tell you as many things as they can about the sticks, using only their eyes to gather information. After a short discussion, ask the children what they think the objects are used for. Tell them the name of the sticks. Ask how many different ways the sticks can be used to produce a sound. The children will probably suggest the following:

- Hit them together hard.
- Tap them together softly.
- Scrape them together.
- Tap the floor or other objects with them.

Accept all of their answers. Let various children demonstrate. Tell them that in a few minutes each of them will be receiving one pair, or two, rhythm sticks to try out. Establish signals that will let the children know when to start or stop making sounds. Pass out the sticks and let the children experiment with them for a few minutes. Signal them to stop. Ask them to lay down their sticks and to listen as you clap out a pattern which you want them to follow. Let children clap it out. For example:

- Clap evenly: 1, 2, 3, 4.
- Clap softly.
- Clap loudly.
- Clap two softly, two loudly.
- Clap two loudly, two softly.
- Clap three softly, one loudly.
- Clap three loudly, one softly.

Ask the children to pick up their sticks and tap out patterns which you name.

On a second occasion, select from a songbook or record a song written in $\frac{4}{4}$ time (4 beats to the measure) and one in which the children can clearly discern the 1, 2, 3, 4 beat. You might use "The Noble Duke of York" or "Skip to My Lou" if these have been taught. Many records lend themselves very nicely to beginning experiences with rhythm instruments; for example, *Gustav's Skoal,* an RCA Victor recording #41-6171, and *Herr Schmidt,* on TNT Records #5004. A series of records that many teachers use in their classrooms is with recording star Hap Palmer and is available from Childcraft or from music stores. Children seem to respond very positively to these.

Procedure: Play the song through for the children to hear. Make sure that the children are comfortable as they listen. You may wish to talk about changes which take place in the music. Ask the children to indicate to you any differences that they hear; the difference may be in the volume or tempo. Have the children clap to the music. Before distributing the sticks, you might also need to remind the children about signals for beginning and ending.

For easy collection of the sticks, use one of several different methods.

- Any girl in the _____ group, please put your sticks away.
- Any boy in the _____ group, please put your sticks away.
- Any girl or boy wearing red, please put your sticks away.
- Any boy wearing buckle shoes come now, please.
- I (or Jill) will come around with the container; please put your pair of sticks in when I come near you (or when Jill comes near you).
- I will call you by name to come and put your sticks away: John, Ellen, Frank, and Melanee, please.

Musical Games
Moving to Music

Song: "My Horses Ain't Hungry," from Seeger's *American Folk Songs for Children,* p. 110.

My horses ain't hungry
They won't eat your hay
So I'll get on my pony,
I'm going away.

Procedure: Teach the song to the children before using it for this activity. Then say, "In the first part of the song, the horses are in the barn; they won't eat the hay. Let me play that part of the music first. When the music changes, the horses are ready to ride away. Let me play all of the song now. You raise your hands when you hear the music change. That's right. The horses aren't hungry and they're riding away. When the music changes, that is your signal to leave the barn.

"Let's divide the class into two groups; the _____ group will be horses in the barn first. What will you need to listen for? The _____ group will sing the song right now; in just a few minutes, they will have a turn to be horses."

After both groups have had a chance to participate, ask the children to describe the horses—their colors, their movements, and the like. Mark on the chalkboard any vocabulary that described how the horses moved, such as *galloped, cantered, walked, ran, trotted, bucked.*

Here Sits a Monkey

Song: "Here Sits a Monkey," from Seeger's *American Folk Songs for Children,* p. 175.

Here sits a monkey in the chair, chair, chair,
He/she lost all the true loves he/she had last year,
So rise upon your feet and greet the first you meet,
The nicest one you know. [I have changed some words.–T.B.]

Procedure: Have the children sit around the edge of the carpet or in a circle on the floor made with chalk or masking tape. (Don't leave tape on the floor for long periods of time as it will ruin the floor.) Teach the children the song first. Place one child on a chair in the middle of the circle. The others walk around the edge of the circle singing the song. When the words "rise upon your feet" are sung, the child on the chair gets up and chooses someone to stand near. This child then sits down in the chair and becomes the monkey. The game begins again.

Musical Chairs

Song: Use a record; marching music or folk songs are appropriate.
Rules: Establish the rules before beginning the game. They are:
- No climbing over the chairs.
- No sitting in a chair until the music stops.
- No saving of seats.
- No pushing or shoving.
- Everyone tries to get a seat.
- The first child in a chair gets the chair.

Procedure: Place a double row of chairs, back to back, diagonally across the room. Use one chair fewer than the number of children. As the music plays, the children move (walk, skip, dance, tiptoe, or march) around the chairs. When the music stops, the children try to find a seat. The child who does not find one leaves the game. Remove one chair each time a child leaves. The child who gets the last chair is the winner.

When there are two children and one chair left, draw a chalk circle around the chair. The two children have to walk on the chalk line while the music plays.

Children who get caught can go to the library center until the time when only two children remain in the game. Bring back all the children to watch the finale.

Spider's Web

Song: "One Little Elephant"

One little elephant went out to play,
On a spider's web one day,

And he/she had such a marvelous time,

That he/she called on another one to get in line.

Procedure: Children form a circle and join hands (the web). One child (the first elephant) stays inside the circle. When the last line of the song is sung, this child selects a child to join him or her and then the two of them weave in and out of the circle under the children's arms. The song continues with "two little elephants" going out to play and continues until all children are in line.

Ideas for Diverse Musical Experiences
Music Appreciation

- Introduce many kinds of music.
- Use music as an integral part of any appropriate social studies unit. Examples: Spain—flamenco music and dance, the guitar, castanets.
  Mexico—the guitar, folk dances.
- Make use of resource people talented in the field of music. Such use might include introduction of various musical instruments, dances, costumes, and folk music.
- Introduce stories set to music. Examples: "Sorcerer's Apprentice," "The Firebird," "Peer Gynt," "Peter and the Wolf," "Swan Lake."
- Study composers and their music.
- Compare different kinds of music.
- Listen and dance to music from foreign countries.
- Listen to many kinds of music from our own country.
- Make up some original songs.
- Use "found" instruments to make music, such as sticks and rocks of various sizes.
- Listen to several folk singers sing their rendition of the same song.
- Act out a musical story.

Interpretations: Free and Directed

Let the children find out the many ways that they can move:

- How many ways can you walk? (Slow, fast; take big steps, little steps; on toes, on heels, on the side of my feet; backwards, frontwards, sideways; toes turned in, toes turned out; sliding walk; one foot in front of the other.)
- How many ways can you go from one place to another? (Run, walk, skate, slide, whirl, crawl, hop, jump, wriggle, roll, somersault, skip; in a crouched position, like an inchworm, spider, or crab; dance.)
- How many ways can you hop? How do grasshoppers, crickets, frogs, toads, rabbits, and kangaroos hop?

Let the children discover various movements which can be made with various parts of their bodies:

- What can your fingers do? How can you move them? your hands? arms? legs, feet, toes, your whole body?

- How many ways can you move while you stay in one place?
  Encourage additional interpretations in these ways:
- As the children move, pick up the rhythm of their movements using sticks, tambourine, or drum.
- Play a record and let the children discuss ideas for movement or what the music makes them think about. You can suggest ideas also.
- The children might think of various animals or themes for music, such as circus, zoo, the ocean, flying, or storms.
- Play two selections which have obvious differences in mood.
- Play simple folk-dance music. Teach simple folk dances.
- Use films, records, filmstrips, and tapes.
- Use music as the basis of a unit of study; for example:
  A Study of Stringed Instruments
  A Study of Ballet
  A Study of a Composer
  A Study of the Guitar
  A Study of Drums
  How Did People First Make Music?
  A Study of Old Instruments
  How Did the Piano Develop?
- Have the children make their own musical instruments.

7.
Study Time

INCLUDED in the kindergarten day is a period of time during which the children's attention is focused on a particular subject. In some classrooms, this period is called "study time." It may occur in a large- or small-group setting. At the beginning of the year study time will be very short, perhaps lasting only ten minutes or so. Gradually lengthen this amount of time so that by mid-November the children will be involved in study for about thirty minutes. Most likely, you will want to conduct study time in a large-group setting for the first three or four weeks of school. Thereafter, you might wish to divide the large group into three smaller groups and keep each group for about fifteen or twenty minutes. Or you may, as some teachers do, feel more comfortable continuing the large-group instruction. I might suggest that alternate arrangements be tried; large-group arrangements are sometimes more appropriate for some activities and small groups better for others. If you choose to make use of the small-group arrangement, it will be necessary to plan carefully so that the children not involved in study can carry on with their activities independently.

In order for any study time to be successful, you will need to make both long- and short-range goals. Planning begins before school starts. The first plans will be for the first week of school. Consider carefully the children who will be in your class and the kinds of experiences they may or may not have had. In some schools, the children arrive having already had several years of nursery school and/or child-care experiences. In other schools the children will not have had any experiences outside the home setting. If your school provides for home visits before school starts, you will have the opportunity to gather important information which will help you with your first plans. If no home visits are made, talk with other teachers at your school. Very often they can provide some insights into the needs of your prospective students. Be sure that your plans for the first days and weeks are flexible enough to allow for either extending, shortening, eliminating, or replacing activities. Plan for more activities than you could possibly include.

The first few weeks of school will provide you with time to gauge the abilities and needs of your students. For example, you may find that most of your children can identify colors, in which case it would be inappropriate to spend three days introducing colors. It would be appropriate, however, to take care of the few children who do still need some additional work in this area and to give many opportunities for all children to extend their knowledge of colors. The latter could be done through the use of films and through experimentation at the art table.

You can make longer-range plans after the first month of school. Some teachers like to plan a month ahead, and others, for one semester.

Content for Study Time

Study-time topics can be drawn from any content area, including social studies, science, mathematics, art, or music. Children especially enjoy studies about animals and food. Alternate topics so that the children's interest can be kept at a high level. The first month might include studies concerned with an animal, color, two-dimensional shapes, and sets. Although most studies cover a five-day period, some will be as short as three days, while others will continue for seven or eight days. It is better psychology to end a study while interest is still high than to extend it for so long that the children become bored with the topic.

In planning a unit of study, consider whether or not the topic will be of interest to the children, if materials are available with which to teach it, and if you are interested in it. Real materials can be augmented by films, filmstrips, pictures, drawings, and models. One of your first steps after determining that materials are available is to check out one or two good children's information books on the topic. It might be wise also to use an encyclopedia. Choose the main ideas that you think are important enough for children to know about. Each of these main ideas will become the focus for one lesson. Your responsibility will be to provide enough materials from which the children can draw information and ideas. For example, if the study is on Teeth, it would be appropriate and helpful to display the skulls of meat- and plant-eating animals along with various food samples. With the proper kinds of questions, the children can be led to discover the relationship which exists between types of teeth and the food eaten. During a study of Insects, display various kinds of common insects so that the children can discover the characteristics common to most insects. If your study focuses on Peanuts, it would be necessary to have peanut plants at various stages of growth in the classroom for the children to observe, peanut pods for each child to examine, and seeds to eat and plant.

Animal Studies

In Chapter III, The First Day, detailed plans for a first study time on Hamsters were discussed. Your first study could be on any pet in your classroom, including a goldfish, guinea pig, mouse, rat, gerbil, or parakeet. Information about the animal which you would want your children to process could include any of the following:

- General description and gross characteristics
- Special characteristics
- Reproductive cycle
- Relatives of the animal
- Food
- Kind of home
- Enemies
- Human uses of the animal
- Geographic location
- Variations in the animal

In order to teach an animal unit, you would need the following:
- The animal in the classroom, if possible, or at some location where the children could have ample opportunity to observe it
- A simple outline drawing of the animal with external parts shown and labels for the parts
- Some pictures or drawings showing special characteristics of the animal
- Pictures of other animals belonging to the same classification as the animal under study
- Pictures or drawings which show variations in the animal (If possible, bring live animals into the classroom which show these variations.)
- Food which the animal eats
- World map
- Products made from the animal
- Skull or skeleton, if possible
- Movies, filmstrips, books
- Drawing or photographs of the home of the animal

Since most young children are interested in animals, you may wish to present animal units throughout the year, perhaps one every four or five weeks. You may want to include an animal from any of the major classifications, such as mammal, bird, fish, insect, crustacean, mollusk, reptile, and arachnid. After studying the general characteristics of animals representative of these classifications, your children will most likely be able to classify other animals.

Following is a complete unit on Hamsters intended to be presented to children over a four- to six-day period. You may need to make some adjustments for your group if you find that some lessons either contain too little or too much content, or too many activities.

A Unit on Hamsters
(See also Chapter III, The First Day.)

First Day. Idea: A hamster is a small fur-covered animal resembling a mouse.

Teacher's Questions (and Activities)	Materials	Children's Activities
What is a hamster? How does it look? Describe its size in relation to a cat, mouse, dog, rabbit. With what is its body covered? What color is its fur? What shape or color are its eyes? What does it have above its mouth? Does it remind you of another animal? Does it make any sounds?	Hamster	Children observe hamster and answer teacher's questions.
How does it feel?		Children feel the fur as teacher brings it around. Some children may be unwilling to touch hamster.
What is a safe way to pick it up?		Children offer their ideas.
(Demonstrate scooping up the hamster using both hands cupped, keeping fingers together.)		Children practice picking up hamster.

Second Day. Idea: The parts of a hamster include head, body, tail, four feet, two eyes, two ears, and whiskers.

Tell me some of the things we found out about the hamster yesterday.	Hamster	Children recall information and describe new observations.
If you observed the hamster this morning, did you notice any additional facts?	Large sample outline drawing of a hamster.	
Let me put the hamster away now. Will you look at the large bulletin board? What do you see there?	Small pieces of paper, each with a design, are stapled near each part of the animal.	Children match designs on pieces of paper with designs or labels naming the parts.

Teacher's Questions (and Activities)	Materials	Children's Activities
We are going to name the parts of the hamster. José, will you find a label which matches this design? Ellen, which part would you like to name? (Continue until all parts are labeled.)		Teacher reads the labels and guides children in labeling activities.
Let me read you a story about a hamster.	Book: Janet Konkle, *J. Hamilton Hamster* (Childrens, ·1957)	

Third Day. Ideas: Hamsters have incisors with which they nibble or gnaw. Hamsters use cheek pouches in which to store food temporarily. The tail is short and furless. The number of toes on front and back feet differs.

We're going to look at our hamster a little more closely today. Let me bring it close to you; please look at its face, tail, and the toes on the front and back feet.	Hamster	Children observe and discuss.
After you've seen the hamster, we'll check my drawing to see if I've made any errors.	Film, if available: *Happy Little Hamsters*, (Portafilms, 1961) Filmstrip: *Rodents*, (Society for Visual Education, Inc., 1967)	
What did you find out about the hamster's tail? How does it look?		
What did you notice about the hamster's toes on the front and back feet?		
Did any of you notice the hamster eating this morning? How did it hold its food?		
Let me give it some food now—watch carefully!	Food: hamster pellets, sunflower seeds, lettuce	

Teacher's Questions (and Activities)	Materials	Children's Activities

What did it do with the food? What happened to its cheeks? Show me how they look.

It has special pockets or pouches in its cheeks. It will keep or hoard the food there until we put it back in the cage. Then it will take it out to eat later.

The word *hamster* comes from a German word meaning "to hoard or keep."

Children talk about the lumps in the cheeks. Children pretend they are hamsters with filled pouches.

If you'll be very quiet, I'll come near you and try to get the hamster to open its mouth so that you can see its teeth. (Firmly stroke downward on its head—be careful not to hurt it.)

Materials: Hamster

How many teeth did you see? How did they look? (If you are squeamish about using this method, use a large drawing of a side view of a hamster's head showing the incisors, or photographs, or a rodent skull, or a film.)

Children relate their observations.

The hamster's teeth are called incisors; its teeth keep growing.

Fourth Day. Idea: A hamster is a rodent. Rodents nibble or gnaw their food with incisors which are constantly growing.

Tell me some of the things you found out about the hamster's teeth yesterday.

Today we'll be using this small bulletin board. Let me read the title. This word says "Rodents."

Materials: Bulletin board titled "Rodents." Included on the board are pictures of a hamster and

Teacher's Questions (and Activities)	Materials	Children's Activities
Can you name some of the animals?	some other rodents, such as mice, rats, guinea pigs, gerbils, beavers.	Children name animals. If unable to, they use a matching procedure as before.
All of these animals have something about them that is the same. Can you tell me what it is? (If children cannot, continue with further questions.) What kind of teeth did our hamster have? How did it eat its food?		
Let me read you a book called *The Lion and the Rat*.	Book: La Fontaine, *The Lion and the Rat* (Franklin Watts, 1963)	
How did the rat save the lion? What did it do to the rope?		
What kind of teeth do you think rats have?		
What is it that all rodents have? That's right, incisors— they gnaw or nibble their food. Remember, their incisors keep growing.		
One of you mentioned you saw the hamster gnawing on its cage. Why might it be doing that? What would happen if the hamster did not grind its teeth down?		
Let's look at our own teeth. (Point out their eight incisors.)		In pairs, children examine each other's teeth.
How are your incisors different from a rodent's incisors?		
What kind of food would be good for a rodent to eat?	Food pellets, carrots	
Is a hamster a rodent? How do you know?		

Teacher's Questions (and Activities)	Materials	Children's Activities

Fifth Day. Idea: A hamster is a mammal.

We've found out a number of interesting things about our hamster. Today we'll find out some other things.

(If a film on hamsters has been seen, ask questions about the life cycle of the hamster. If no film is available, use drawings and pictures of mammals, including the hamster, feeding their young; or use a book with many illustrations.)

How were hamster babies born? Were they in an egg?

Who cared for the babies and fed them? What was their first food? How did the young look? Did they have any fur? Tell me about their eyes.

How many young were born?

This bulletin board is titled "Mammals." What do you notice about the baby animals? Where are they getting their food? How do they look?

Most animals which bear live young and feed them milk from their bodies are called mammals.

Can you name some mammals you know?

Are you a mammal? How do you know?

We have found out that a hamster is both a mammal and a rodent!

Film: *Happy Little Hamsters,* or pictures of mammals, some feeding their young, on a bulletin board titled "Mammals." Include pictures of a hamster, dog, cat, pig, cow, and people.

Children observe and answer teacher's questions.

Additional Activities	Materials	Children's Activities
If you wish, draw attention to the fact that there are different kinds of hamsters, either by bringing varieties into the classroom or by displaying their pictures.		
You may also wish to have the children see where hamsters originally came from.	World map, yarn	On the world map, children identify Syria, and place a small drawing of a hamster in that area of the map. They then attach a piece of yarn connecting Syria and the area in which you live.

Evaluation

Evaluate what the children have learned by asking them to draw a hamster, using all the space on an 8½ × 11″ or 9 × 12″ paper, and to tell you about their drawing. If the children are reluctant or seem unsure, ask questions to provoke discussion of what they have learned. Print the children's stories on their pictures and display them in your room.

For the very reluctant child, point out and discuss the basic shapes that form the head, body, legs, and tail of the hamster.

Accept all drawings, but do not accept erroneous information. Help each child discern errors in his or her story.

Other Animal Units

Depending on your locale, the season, library or naturalist resources, and your own knowledge, you may want to study any of a large number of animals. Following are some that have been interesting to children in my experience. If you want to study a number of animals, you may want to choose no more than one from a classification, to begin to help children build an awareness of the wide diversity of living things. If you want to study only two or three you can also choose from within a classification, to develop a deeper understanding of the characteristics those animals share.

Classification	Animals		
Mammals	• Rabbit	• Monkey	• Squirrel
	• Guinea pig	• Whale	• Cat (domestic or wild)

Classification	Animals		
Mammals (*Continued*)	• Gerbil • Cow	• Porpoise • Raccoon	
Birds	• Robin • Cardinal • Sparrow	• Blue jay • Parrot • Mockingbird	• Parakeet • Canary
Bird of Prey	• Hawk	• Owl	• Eagle
Reptile	• Snake • Turtle	• Dinosaur • Alligator	• Lizard
Amphibian	• Toad • Frog	• Salamander • Newt	
Fish	• Bass • Trout • Flounder	• Shark • Tropical fish of various kinds	• Goldfish
Insect	• Cricket • Grasshopper • Dragonfly	• Bee • Ant • Butterfly	• Moth • Mosquito • Fly
Marsupial	• Kangaroo	• Opossum	
Crustacean	• Lobster	• Crayfish	• Crab
Mollusk	• Snail • Oyster	• Clam • Octopus	• Whelk • Squid
Arachnid	• Spider	• Scorpion	
Rodent	• Mouse • Rat	• Guinea pig • Squirrel	• Beaver • Hamster

Food Studies

It is no secret that young children especially enjoy units which involve cooking and eating experiences. These units are valuable for many reasons: they provide many opportunities to introduce or reinforce mathematical concepts, to introduce new language, to teach and practice social skills, and to teach the nutritional value of foods.

Units taught early in the year should be simple studies, such as a study of apples, some kind of squash, or green peppers. You might devote four study periods to one of these topics. Units on corn, peanuts, bananas, or chocolate can be taught after a couple months of school. It might be appropriate to teach a unit on corn after a study of Mexico.

Following is an outline of a food unit which might serve as a model for a unit you may wish to develop yourself.

A Unit on Apples

First Day. Idea: An apple is a red, round, edible fruit. It has seeds contained within its core.

Teacher's Questions (and Activities)	Materials	Children's Activities
What do I have in my hand? Can you describe it for me?	One red apple	Children observe the apple and answer questions.
If I wanted to find out some more things about the apple, what could I do?	Knife	Children give their ideas.
(Pare off some skin.) What do you see now? What else might I do? (Cut it in half.) What do you see now?		
I'm going to cut these apples in two so that each of you will have an equal part. How much will you have?	One apple for each two children	
When you get your half, would you examine it very closely? (Give children a few minutes.) What did you notice?		Children examine their halves and discuss their observations.
Where are the seeds? Why? Did they have protection? Describe the seeds. How many did you find?		

Teacher's Questions (and Activities)	Materials	Children's Activities

You may smell your apple now. How does it smell?

How else can we find out some more about the apple? Yes, you may eat it. Tell me what you discovered.

Second Day. Idea: The parts of an apple are the skin, meat or flesh, core, seeds, and stem.

Teacher's Questions	Materials	Children's Activities
Today we're going to use our bulletin board. What do you see there? We're going to name the parts of an apple.	A large two-dimensional model of an apple—perhaps 24 × 24". Make it in layers, so that as children name a part it can be removed to reveal the next layer or part. Labels for the parts.	Children match labels to the parts of the apple.
(Show parts on the real apple as they are labeled on the bulletin board.)	A real apple	

Idea: Apples grow on apple trees.

(If you have a filmstrip or film showing the life cycle of an apple, use it; otherwise, present the sequence using drawings or cutouts.) My pictures tell a story. Can you tell where to begin? How did you know? What happened first? Next? Third? Fourth? Fifth?	Film or filmstrip on life cycle of apples. A series of pictures showing: 1. seed in the ground 2. seed germinating into small plant	Children describe which picture is next in the sequence and describe what they see.

Teacher's Questions (and Activities)	Materials	Children's Activities
	3. young tree 4. tree in blossom 5. tree with apples	
(At story time, read *Johnny Appleseed*.)	Book: Eva Moore, *Johnny Appleseed* (Scholastic Book Services, 1970)	

Third Day. Idea: Apples can be used in many different ways.

All of the items you see on the table were made from apples. The title on the board reads "What Can You Do With Apples?"	Display of items made from apples. Examples: apple juice or cider, applesauce, and candied apple. Pictures of apple pie, apple dumpling, and baked apples.	
Can you tell me some of the ways we use apples? Is there something that your mother does with apples that we have not talked about?		Children use boards and display to answer teacher's questions.
I'll come around and give each of you some canned applesauce.	Small paper cups, two for each child.	
Tomorrow we'll make our own. Now, each of you will get a taste of apple juice.		

Teacher's Questions (and Activities)	Materials	Children's Activities

Fourth Day. Idea: Applesauce is made by peeling, cutting up, and cooking apples that have been sweetened with sugar.

Teacher's Questions (and Activities)	Materials	Children's Activities
(During self-chosen time provide children with potato peelers. Let each child have a turn peeling. Cut and core the apples. Show the children how they look.)	Apples, sugar, water, cinnamon, red hots, pot, hot plate, large spoon, potato peelers. A recipe for applesauce.	
(Read the recipe to the children.)		
(Let the apples cook as children participate in self-chosen activities.)		Children measure out amounts of cut-up apple, sugar, water, and cinnamon. Teacher adds a few red hots for color.
What do you think will happen as the apples cook?		Children give their ideas.
(Cool!)		
(At study time, share applesauce with children.) How does it look now? How have the apples changed? How does it smell?	Small paper cups, plastic spoons.	Children eat their applesauce.
Let's eat!		

Fifth Day. Idea: There are many kinds of apples.

Teacher's Questions (and Activities)	Materials
The kind of apple we examined and cooked was a _____ .	Examples of various kinds of apples:
Let's see if someone can find an apple like it on our table.	Golden Delicious, Red Delicious,
_____ , will you try?	Granny Apples, Spies,
How did you know?	McIntosh,
What do you see on the table?	Rome Beauty, Winesap.

Teacher's Questions (and Activities)	Materials	Children's Activities
How are they alike? How are they different?	Labels for each. Pictures on a bulletin board if real apples not available.	Children discuss similarities and differences.
Let's use our eyes, nose, and mouth to help us.		Children eat small samples of each kind, comparing appearance, odor, texture, and taste.

More Complex Ideas
More complicated concepts can be taught if you wish, such as *where* apples are grown in the United States and *why* and *which* states produce the most apples. This learning might be more appropriate later in the year after some units on maps and weather have been presented. At this time, if you are asked why apples are not grown in your state, you might simply say, "We do not have the right kind of weather to grow apples."

Other Food Studies

Other food studies might center around corn, bread, squash, bananas, oranges, green peppers, watermelons, cantaloupes, peas, vanilla, cinnamon, chocolate, peanuts, pumpkin, butter, cranberries, tea, cheese, onions, ice cream, coffee, pecans, walnuts, salt, water, pineapples, and milk.

8.
Resource People

A variety of approaches to the study of any topic leads to increased involvement and learning for both students and teacher. The use of resource people is a way to enrich your program and enhance any area of the curriculum.

Resource people can be parents, other students, teachers, nonteaching staff at school, and members of the community.

Parents

Information concerning talents or special interests of parents can be gathered during a home visit, from forms sent home to parents, during conference time, or while parents attend school meetings. I have found that many parents are willing to act as resource people, but that they are not sure that they will know how to talk to a class of young children. These fears are generally alleviated if you tell them to:

• keep their presentation down to 10-20 minutes
• talk to the children in a normal tone, speaking as they would to another adult
• bring real objects to show the children.

Be sure to let them know that you will be there to guide the learning experience and to manage the children. Offer some suggestions for the sequence of the presentation. Tell them that you would like to have the children ask questions at the end of the presentation.

In my classroom, parents have served as resource people to enhance the following units:

Parent	Unit
Orthopedic surgeon	Bones
Anthropologist	Masks
Doctor	Blood
Geologist	Rocks and Minerals
Mexican national	Mexico

Amateur beekeeper	Bees
Australian national	Australia
Art professor	Printmaking
Zoologist	Lizards
Banker, Coin collector	Money
Contractor	Homes
Ballet dancer	Ballet
University professor	Israel
University professor	Holland

Other Students

Students in your school represent a pool of untapped sources from which resource people can be drawn. Your children will respond well to older students who might be able to share specific art projects, musical instruments, or dance forms and costumes, among many other possibilities. If you are fortunate enough to have children from other countries in your school, let them share information about games, toys, holidays, customs, sports, schools, dress, and foods.

The School Staff

Resource people can often be found among the teaching staff, the office personnel, and the library, cafeteria, and custodial staff. For example, if a unit on Leaders or Rules is being presented, learning sequences could involve interviews with the principal, the cafeteria manager, the head of the custodial staff, or the head librarian. A unit on Our School could use representatives from the office, cafeteria, library, custodial staff, special-education staff, special-area teaching staff, and primary or intermediate levels. Individuals with special talents or interests could be invited to visit the classroom. You might find a musician, a singer of folk songs, a well-seasoned traveler with souvenirs from other countries, or a gourmet cook. Some recent visitors in my class included:

Staff Member	Topic Discussed
Custodian	Making a purse out of a bleach bottle with crocheting
Custodian	Growing tobacco
Custodian	Needlepoint and embroidery
Librarian	Caldecott Awards Information on the monarch butterfly
Art teacher	Weaving Use of the potter's wheel

Cafeteria manager	Baking bread and rolls
Teacher	Playing the guitar
Student teachers	Introducing the banjo and the trumpet
Student	Introducing and playing the violin
Office staff member	Knitting
Custodian	Handling the flag

The Community

The community offers rich resources if you are willing to seek them out. The children can be taken to specific locations or visitors from the community can be invited to the school. You might use the following resources to enrich the study units thus:

Resource	Unit
Shoe store	Shoes
Grocery store or a home garden	Roots We Eat
Grocery store	Vines
Grocery store	Citrus Fruits
Dairy or dairy farm	Milk
Dairy	Ice Cream
Dairy	Butter
Dentist's office	Dentistry and Teeth
Dentist's office, beauty shop, furniture store, shoe store, office	Chairs
Clock store	Clocks
Neighborhood	Houses
Neighborhood	Fences
Local folk-dance group	Folk Dances
Museum	Fossils
Science museum, pet shop, or aquarium	Animals
Cement truck visiting at school	Concrete
Water-purifying plant	Water
Dam	Dams
River	Rivers
Boat factory or shipyard, if available	Boats
Bridges	Bridges
Potter's studio	Pottery, Clay

Neighborhood	Doors
Bank, coin store, variety store, grocery; armored truck visiting at school	Money
Bakery, mill	Bread
Book bindery, public or school library	Books

9.
Room Management

THE questions which new teachers ask most often are generally related to room management or discipline. The frequency with which these questions surface reveals the uncertainty and fears that many new teachers feel when they think about walking into, and taking charge of, their very own classroom on the first day of school. Their concerns are usually expressed in one of the following ways:

- How will I manage a whole roomful of children?
- How do I get them to do what I say?
- What do I do if they won't?

The most important factor which contributes to successful classroom management is the teacher—his or her behavior, personality, and attitude toward the teaching role.

Successful classrooms evolve when there is a teacher who:

- Is very natural and does not take on a different personality when working with children.
- Does not use a special voice or talk down to children.
- Is friendly, warm, and kind, but is not a "pal" to the students.
- Remains in charge of the room and does not relinquish this responsibility to the students.
- Is fair and just with all of the children, treating each one with respect, kindness, and courtesy.
- Is not quick to blame when behavior breaks down, but seeks fair and just solutions for problems that arise.
- Sets up and maintains reasonable standards of behavior from the first day of school.
- Establishes classroom routines early in the year, so that the children know what is expected of them.
- Feels and exhibits at appropriate times and in appropriate amounts a wide range of emotions.
- Will admit that she or he is human and can make errors.
- Is flexible.
- Remains a learner.

- Is a reader who shows by example his or her interest in and love of books.
- Maintains a supportive classroom environment, one in which children feel comfortable enough to try to answer questions or to find solutions for problems.
- Strives to provide successful experiences for all students.
- Listens to children when they talk to her or him.
- Keeps an attractive classroom, one which is inviting to children.
- In setting up the classroom, takes into account such things as safety, traffic patterns, the kinds of activities and materials which will be included, and the number of children who can work in any one area.
- Offers a variety of activities, alternating those which require students to sit fairly quietly and to follow the teacher's directions with those which allow more freedom of movement and choice of activity.
- Changes displays, materials, and equipment often enough to keep interest high.
- Has available enough materials and equipment for the number of children in the classroom.
- Is willing to expend the kind of energy necessary to provide a stimulating learning environment.
- Uses teaching strategies which conform with the way young children learn.
- Makes long- and short-range plans, but realizes that sometimes the needs of the children or his or her own needs will necessitate changes in those plans.

When Behavior Breaks Down

Because most children come to school wanting to do what's right and what is expected of them, the task of managing a classroom is less difficult than what it may seem. However, there will be times when behavior will break down and problems will occur. The best advice that can be given to a new teacher is: try to remain calm, listen to the child or children involved as carefully as possible, and try to come up with a fair solution to the problem. If a child has been hurt, by all means take care of the medical need first. If a child or the children are too upset to talk out the problem, be patient and wait until they are ready to do so. If children become so angry that they cannot control themselves, try to isolate them or leave them for a few minutes until they can regain control. Since there is generally a loss of face with fellow students when such outbursts occur, a few minutes in a private place allow the children time to recover. Some teachers prefer to talk privately to any students involved in an altercation; they will take the child into the hallway or a corner of the room to talk things over. If you try this approach, you will find that the rest of your students will want to observe and to listen to all that goes on. You might say, "This is something that Carol and JoAnn need to work out together with my help. Would you please go back to work?" Or, "John and Andy are not very happy right now. We need to talk it over privately. I will be back with you in just a few minutes." Or, "These children have had a misunderstanding; we are going to see if we can find a solution to the problem. I'll be back in the classroom shortly."

If the child becomes angry and uses abusive language, try to remain calm and avoid raising your voice. *Don't argue with the child.* You might say in a firm, clear voice, "I know that you are angry with me right now and that's all right, but you cannot talk to me that way." Or, "I can tell you didn't like what I did just now, and I am sorry that you feel that way. I didn't like the words that I heard just now and don't want to hear them in the classroom again."

After speaking to the child, walk away. Give the child time to recuperate from this breakdown in behavior.

Very often it is wise simply to observe for a few minutes the children who are involved in an argument. Frequently you will find that children will discover solutions themselves, without adult intervention. If safety is involved, don't hesitate.

One of the most important rules to follow is to be consistent in dealing with behavior which is not in accordance with standards that have been set up for the classroom. Nothing confuses children more than a teacher who overlooks certain negative behaviors on some occasions and reacts strongly to the same behaviors at other times. Trust is built up between the students and the teacher when the students know that the same rules exist for every member of the class and that the teacher can be depended upon to enforce class rules fairly and equitably at all times. In the beginning of the school year, a few important rules are set up; these usually pertain to safety and to classroom routines. Other rules can be added if and when they are needed. If you want to make a chart, stress positive behaviors:

In This Classroom, We Have Students Who:
- Work together
- Learn together
- Share materials and ideas
- Help each other
- Respect one another

or

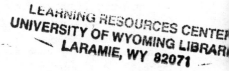

Our Teacher Tells Us That We Are:
- Good Workers
- Careful Listeners
- Creative Thinkers
- Good Sports

The chart can be completed as a cooperative art project with various children assigned to illustrate specific characteristics. Another idea is to have the children make individual drawings illustrating their ideas. After stories are printed on them, the drawings can be displayed on a bulletin board or made into a class book.

When Little Things Annoy

Days will exist when you will not be feeling well enough to withstand the normal noise or movement in the classroom. On these occasions it is perfectly all right to let the children know how you feel. You might say, "I'm not feeling too well today. I would really appreciate it very much if you could lower your voices a bit and be a little quieter as you move about the room." Or, "Would you please work a little quieter today? I'm not feeling too well. Thank you." Or, "I have a headache today and I really need less noise in the room." Or, "I need a few quiet moments for myself. I'd really appreciate your help. Would you take care of yourselves for a little while?"

Establishing Authority

In the first few minutes of the first day of school, you will begin to establish or undermine your credibility as the teacher in charge of the classroom. As the children arrive, they will be looking to you for direction, watching for clues which will tell them about their teacher and what kinds of behaviors will be allowed in the classroom. When you speak to the children on the first day and every other day, expect that they will listen and do what you say. First days are very special days for young children; meeting their new teacher is very exciting. Most will want to please you and will comply with your requests. For the reluctant few, your task will be a little more difficult and will require persistence and consistency on your part. There are children who, for some reason, seem to feel that they must test any new authority figure. The testing may be of short duration, lasting only a day or two, or it may continue on and off throughout the year. Children who display the latter kind of behavior seem to benefit most from firmness, fairness, and consistency in teacher behavior. If a child does continue to test in a stable environment, it might be well to ask for additional help in dealing with the problem. You might talk with the parents, former teachers, principal or head teacher, or a psychometrist or psychologist. Of course, parental permission would have to be granted for any testing to be done.

Before making any requests of the children, consider the reasonableness of the request. Ask yourself:

- Can the child do it?
- Is it important and necessary that it be done?
- Does the child have the materials with which to do it?
- Is there adequate time and space within which it can be done?

If the answers are yes, make the request and be sure to follow through on it. When making a request, use a voice that carries the message that you expect your request to be carried out—which does not mean using a loud or authoritarian voice, but a normal speaking voice, with the words spoken rather matter-of-factly.

Threats

Very often teachers will include the threat of some form of punishment when making requests or giving directions to children. The threat might include the loss of a privilege; nonparticipation in certain activities; or informing parents, principal, or head teacher. Hopefully, the threat of physical punishment would not be made or carried out. The wisest approach would be to exclude the use of threats. As was stated earlier, if you expect good behavior from your students and have been fair with them, it is more than likely that you will not be disappointed. One of the problems with using threats is that to insure credibility, noncompliance must be met with the threatened action. For example, if you say to a child, "Would you please not run around the room?" and then add, "If you don't, you will have to lose part of your free time," it would be necessary to see that this is indeed what does happen if the child continues to run about the room.

Some teachers use threats which the children know cannot be carried out. For example, if you say, "If you don't quiet down, we will not go to lunch" and your school has a rigid lunchhour schedule, the children know that your words are meaningless. As substitute behavior, you might try complimenting children who are obviously ready to leave for lunch. For example, say, "I am very glad I have children in this room who know that it is time for us to go to lunch. They are helping us get ready to leave by being quiet." If you are observant, you will probably notice that the larger proportion of your class is ready to comply with your request. Leave the room, walking briskly, staying beside the one or two children who are having trouble settling down. You might hold their hands.

Unhappily, very often it is the child who needs most *not* to miss study times, outdoor play times, or opportunities to work with other children who seems less able to conform to room standards of behavior. If you respond to misbehavior by removing the child from various activities very often, the child not only misses valuable experiences, but might also begin to take on a more negative self-opinion. The class might begin to label the child as the one who always gets in trouble. To avoid this kind of pattern, make the best start possible in managing your classroom. Set up the few rules necessary to maintain a healthy room environment, be consistent in adhering to the rules, and deal with the children fairly.

Punishment

There is another trap to avoid in dealing with children's misbehavior. In the first few weeks of school, it would be inadvisable to use what I would consider the most serious teacher punishment—putting the child out of the classroom. If you resort to this punishment early in the year, where do you go from there? During the early weeks, I would try various methods. For some children, a glance or a spoken reminder is sufficient. For others, just saying their name will do the trick. Some children respond to a whispered message in their ear or a touch on their heads. If a child is disruptive at study time after being asked to stop, you might try one of the following:

• Get up, walk over to the child, and tell the child very quietly but firmly that you need for him or her to be quiet.
• Move the child to a different location.
• Bring the child up very close to where you are seated so that you can touch the child to remind him or her of your expectations for behavior.

- Move the child from the group, perhaps just a foot or so away.

After dealing with any child's misbehavior, go on with your lesson. Occasionally, a child who has been moved or has received special teacher attention for misbehavior will be embarrassed in front of the group and, to save face, may make faces or gestures. Try as best you can to ignore this kind of behavior. If a child cries, you might move the child close to you; comfort him or her a little, but continue your lesson. You might say, "I am sorry if I upset you; I do need your help to make this a good study." Do not exclude the child from the study.

If a child continues not to respond to reasonable requests for appropriate behavior during these first few weeks, it may be necessary to remove some privileges, such as:
- loss of 5-10 minutes of free time
- loss of 5-10 minutes of outdoor-play time
- nonparticipation in one game

Let the child know why any privileges have been lost.

Playground Injuries

Even though you have set up a few basic rules for safety, on occasion a child will throw a stone, hit or poke someone with a stick, or knock a playmate down. Since it is almost impossible to see all that goes on every minute during outdoor-play time, very often you will have no way of knowing whether it was an accident, an intentional act, or the result of provocation. If a child has been hurt, take care of the medical needs first. Speak to all of the children who were involved. You might say, "Stones are not for throwing and people are not for hurting. I need everyone to play safely. I would appreciate your help."

If there is a recurrence of the same behavior by the same child, it is probable that the act was not accidental. If you're very angry, you might say, "I am feeling very angry right now. Would you please just sit beside me until I feel calmer. Then we will talk." After you have calmed down, you might say, "Since we have already talked together once before today, I believe that I need for you to stay with me for a little while. The other children need to feel safe while they play. I cannot let them get hurt." You might keep the child sitting for about ten minutes. It may be necessary to have the child play near you for a day or two until you are sure that the child can be mindful of others on the playground.

Poor Resters

Because many children who come to school no longer have a rest or nap at home, they have difficulty settling down at rest time—which can create some problems for you if your daily schedule includes a rest period. Some suggestions for helping the children adjust to the rest period are (for additional information, see Rest Time in Chapter III):

- Find some quiet work to do that will not require *you* to move about the room as the children rest.
- Read stories or play story records for the children. In the beginning of the year, select short stories and use stories familiar to the children. Folk tales such as "Hansel and Gretel," "Little Red Riding Hood," "Rumpelstilskin," "Jack and the Beanstalk," "The Three Billy Goats Gruff," and "The Three Bears" are appropriate. Weston Woods (Weston, Connecticut 06880) has many fine records from which you can choose. As the year progresses, children will be able to listen to longer stories.
- If a child consistently disturbs others, it may be necessary to move the child's cot or rest mat to a corner of the room or near you until the child feels that he or she can be quiet.
- When children are positioning their cots or mats, you may wish to rearrange a few. Some children do less visiting and rest better away from their best friends.

Dealing with Poor Eating Habits

In your classroom you may find children who:
- want to eat the dessert first
- eat only the dessert
- drink liquids but do not eat solid foods
- are unwilling to try any new foods
- tell you they are allergic to certain foods
- eat very small amounts
- gulp down their food
- want to eat what's on everybody else's plates or in others' lunchboxes
- display table behaviors which you deem unacceptable

Some of these problems are easier to solve than others.

To avoid the problem of so-called allergies to food, it is a simple matter to send home a short form asking the parents to list any food allergy or special diet their child has. This kind of information can be included on a preregistration form. To get you additional information about the children's food habits, other questions can be asked on a home visit or answered on a form.

Early in the year, the children and you can talk about and list some appropriate cafeteria behaviors. If a chart is made, try to stress positive behaviors:

In Our Cafeteria We:

- enjoy eating together
- visit quietly
- try new foods
- help each other
- eat dessert last if it's ice cream, pudding, cake, cookies, or candy
- eat dessert with our lunch if it is fruit or jello

Let the children draw pictures to illustrate these ideas. If you think it's appropriate, you might have the children discuss and decide on penalties for not conforming to the agreed-on behaviors.

If the children ask you if they have to eat everything on their plate, have an answer ready for them. You could say: "Let's all agree to try everything that's on our plate, even if it's something new. You'll never know how it tastes unless you try it. If after trying it you find that you don't like it, you may leave it. I am going to ask you to eat some of everything and to drink some milk. I think that would be fair. I can't tell you when you've had enough— you'll know that yourself. You decide."

If you have children who consistently eat very little of the hot meal, I would suggest speaking to the parents to find out what their lunch usually consists of at home. Very often, a child is used to eating a peanut-butter or bologna sandwich and drinking a glass of milk. In some cases, the food which is eaten at home is quite different from that which is served at school. You might suggest to the parents that their child bring lunch from home on three days of the week and eat the school lunch the remaining two. In this arrangement, the child gets enough to eat and still has the experience of trying new foods while sharing a hot lunch with classmates.

Most teachers would be surprised at the limited diet of many young children. To encourage children to be willing to try new foods, teach food units and social-studies units on foreign countries, including the preparation, cooking, and eating of a wide variety of foods. You will find that most children will try a bite of foods they have prepared themselves. Start out studying foods that are familiar to the children. Party times will afford you additional opportunities to let the children try new recipes and have new tasting experiences.

By the end of the school year, you will be pleasantly surprised at the many changes that will have taken place with the children.

Checklist for Danger Signs

If you find that you are reprimanding children very often and that there is much discord in your room, it might be well for you to analyze why this is happening. Ask yourself the following questions.

- Do I have too many rules?
- Are the rules too restrictive?
- Am I asking the children to do things which are beyond their capabilities? For example, am I asking the children to sit still too long?
- Am I watching the children too closely and reprimanding them for behavior which is quite appropriate and not unusual for young children?
- Are class rules fairly applied?
- Are there enough activities to keep the children involved?
- Are the activities which I offer sufficiently interesting and challenging?
- Do I have a variety of materials and equipment? Are they appropriate for young children?
- Are there opportunities for every child to shine?

Note: Reread the checklist for successful classrooms on the first pages of this chapter.

Epilogue

THE main purpose of *Kindergarten Minute by Minute* is twofold—to share the kind of information that would help new teachers of young children to get off to a good start, and also to allay some of the anxieties felt by them about teaching their first class of children. Certainly, the information contained in the various chapters can be put to good use by the not-so-new teachers as well.

This book was not intended to replace, but to coexist with materials or curriculum guides already available to the teacher. Many teachers are given general guides which offer suggestions for art, music, literature, games, and a unit or two generally related to a holiday or a seasonal theme. These guides are useful. I would suggest that after the first few weeks are over, you examine them and choose activities from among those offered which will fit the needs of the children best.

The chapters in this book devoted to music and art, and the finger plays, transitional activities, and book list found in the Appendix supplement any general guide. The book probably supplies enough ideas for art activities to take care of an entire year's art program. The suggestions contained in Chapter VI, Music, serve as a guide for the kinds of musical activities appropriate for young children. The two units in Chapter VII, Study Time, serve as models for units that you yourself will develop. First-grade teachers might also find all of these chapters helpful in planning activities for six-year-olds.

Some schools provide curricular materials for the various content areas such as mathematics, social studies, science, and oral-language development. Perhaps the most valuable suggestion that I might make would be to examine these materials after school has started and to ask the following questions during your review.

- Is ample time taken to teach basic concepts—concepts on which more complex and abstract concepts will be built?
- Are there opportunities for children to meet the same concept many times and in a variety of ways?
- Are the experiences designed to teach children basic concepts in a way appropriate to how young children learn?

- Are there provisions made for children to manipulate materials, to have real experiences, and to see real things?
- Are there opportunities for children to do lots of talking and questioning?
- Does the teacher's guide describe various levels of questions and emphasize the importance of asking many questions as children work?
- Are the experiences organized in an orderly, sequential way, with more difficult concepts occurring later in the program?
- Is there more emphasis on the use of manipulatives than on paper-and-pencil tasks?
- Has there been a strong attempt to relate the content to other subject-matter areas?

If all of these questions can be answered in the affirmative, chances are that the materials are appropriate for young children. If the answer is no to any of these questions, then I would suggest that you modify the activities and experiences until an affirmative answer can be obtained.

One last word! The first year of teaching is probably the most rewarding, the most exciting, and the most frustrating. It is a year of learning not only for the children but for you as well. Just as children are revising, refining, or strengthening concepts, so do you have the opportunity to test concepts learned while preparing to be a teacher. I would hope that you will be revising, refining, and strengthening concepts in light of the new experiences offered in the daily life of your classroom.

To remain a learner is to be a successful and happy teacher.

Appendix

Finger Plays

F INGER plays have an almost magical effect on young children, particularly at the beginning of the year. If you start a finger play when children are having difficulty settling down for a directed time, in just a few moments they will either be participating or be simply entranced by the words and motions. Finger plays seem to have a soothing effect on unhappy children and to give comforting reassurance to shy children. Because of these reasons, I have often thought of finger plays as related to nursery rhymes, which provide such joyous moments to young children.

Sources of Finger Plays

Finger plays are passed on from teacher to teacher in the same way that folk songs were passed along long ago. The ones included in this section have been learned from teachers over the years, and if they once had an author, that authorship has long been forgotten.

Note: Don't overuse finger plays. They are most appreciated when used occasionally. They are not meant to supplant poetry.

Animal Finger Plays

My bunny's so funny,

It wiggles its nose

And then hops away on the tips of its toes.

Motions: Use index and middle finger for ears. Hold thumb and ring finger together and wiggle for nose. Use index and middle finger to hop away on tips.

I had a little turtle,

It always walked so slow,

For if it walked any faster

It'd be sure to stub its toe. Ouch!

Motions: Hold left arm out and walk up it with index and middle fingers of right hand. When you come to the last word, slide your fingers down arm to hand.

Here is the beehive

But where are the bees?

Hiding away where nobody sees.

Now they come creeping out of the hive

One, two, three, four, five.

BZZZZZZZZZZZZZZZZZZZ!

Motions: Cup the hand into a fist. Starting with thumb, extend fingers one by one as you count.

Ten little kittens standing in a row,

They bow their heads to the children so.

They run to the left, they run to the right,

They stand up and stretch with all their might.

Along comes a dog who wants some fun.

Meow, meow,

Just see those kittens run.

Motions: Use ten fingers to represent kittens. Use one hand to represent dog and then ten fingers again for the running kittens.

Five little chickadees

Peeping at the door.

One flew away

And then there were four.

Chorus

Chickadee, chickadee, happy and gay,

Chickadee, chickadee, fly away.

Four little chickadees

Sitting in a tree.

One flew away

And then there were three.

Three little chickadees

Looking at you.

One flew away

And then there were two.

Two little chickadees

Sitting in the sun.

One flew away
And then there was one.

One little chickadee
Left all alone.
It flew away
And then there were none.

Motions: Use fingers to represent five birds. Take one finger away at a time.

Five little squirrels sitting in a tree
The first one said, What's that I see?
The second said, I smell a gun,
The third one said, Let's run, run, run,
The fourth one said, Let's sit in the shade,
The fifth one said, I'm not afraid.
Then bang went the gun, and how those squirrels did run!

This little froggie broke his toe,
This little froggie said, Oh, Oh, Oh!
This little froggie laughed and was glad,
This little froggie cried and was sad,
This little froggie did what he should,
He hopped for a doctor as fast as he could.

Five little bunnies sitting at the door,
One hopped away and then there were four.
Four little bunnies sitting under a tree,
One hopped away and then there were three.
Three little bunnies looking at you,
One hopped away and then there were two.
Two little bunnies sitting in the sun,
One hopped away and then there was one.
One little bunny left all alone,
It hopped away and then there was none.

This little cow eats grass,
This little cow eats hay,
This little cow drinks water,
This little cow runs away,
This little cow does nothing but lie in the grass all day.

Motions: Show one finger at a time as you talk about each cow.

Funny, funny bunny, hop, hop, hop.

Funny, funny bunny, stop, stop, stop.

Funny, funny bunny, run and play.

Funny, funny bunny, don't run away.

Motions: Use index and middle fingers to show hopping motion. (Tips of fingers touch floor or other surface.)

Five little mocking birds sitting in a tree

The first one said, What's that I see?

The second one said, See a lady up the street!

The third one said, She's putting out seeds.

The fourth one said, Seeds are good to eat!

The fifth one said, Tweet, tweet, tweet!

Motions: Show one finger at a time for each of the five birds. Start with thumb.

Eensy teensy spider went up the water spout,

Down came the rain and washed the spider out.

Out came the sun and dried up all the rain

And the teensy weensy spider

Went up the spout again.

Motions: Touch index finger of right hand to thumb of left hand, then thumb of right hand to index finger of left hand. Repeat to show climbing motion of spider. Make circle with arms for sun.

Two little blackbirds sitting on a hill,

One named Jack, the other named Jill.

Fly away, Jack; fly away, Jill,

Come back, Jack; come back, Jill.

Motions: Hold up index finger of each hand. Put one hand behind back for "Fly away, Jack," and put other hand behind back for "Fly away, Jill." Bring one hand in front for "Come back, Jack," and the other one in front for "Come back, Jill."

Three little ducks that I once knew,

Short ones, fat ones, and skinny ones too,

But the one little duck with the feather on its back

It ruled the others with its quack, quack, quack.

Down to the river they would go

Wiggle waggle, wiggle waggle to and fro,

But the one little duck with the feather on its back
It ruled the others with its quack, quack, quack!

Motions: Show three fingers. Use hands to show various sizes. For "the one little duck," show one finger and hold index and middle finger of other hand behind head. Put palms together and wiggle back and forth for ducks walking to the river.

There was a turtle and it lived in a box,
It swam in a puddle and it climbed on the rocks,
It snapped at a mosquito and it snapped at a flea,
It snapped at a minnow and it snapped at me!
It caught the mosquito and it caught the flea,
It caught the minnow but it didn't catch me!

A little mouse hid in a hole
Quietly in a hole, shhhhhh!
When all was safe as safe could be,
Out popped he!

Motions: Put closed hand inside the other. Take it out and wiggle fingers.

Here is a turkey with its tail spread wide,
It sees the farmer coming, so it's trying to hide.
It runs across the barnyard, wobble, wobble, wobble,
Talking turkey talk, gobble, gobble, gobble.

Motions: Spread fingers wide, put thumb in front for turkey's head. Hide thumb with fingers. Wiggle hand back and forth for running motion.

Finger positions for turkey finger play

With its tail spread wide
So it's trying to hide

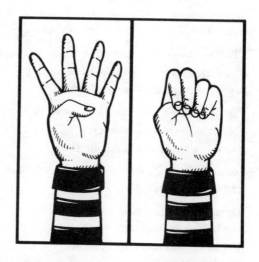

Come, my bunnies, it's time for bed—
That's what the mother bunny said.
But first I'll count you just to see
If you have all come back to me.
Bunny 1, bunny 2, bunny 3 so dear,
Bunny 4, bunny 5, yes you're all here.
You're the sweetest things alive,
My dear little bunnies, 1, 2, 3, 4, 5.

Creeping, creeping, creeping, comes the little cat,
But bunny with long ears hops like that.

Motions: Walk two fingers on one arm and then hop down the other arm with two fingers.

There was a bunny who lived in the woods,
It wiggled its ears like a good bunny should.
It hopped by a squirrel, it hopped by a tree,
It hopped by a duck and it hopped by me.
It stared at the squirrel, it stared at the tree,
It stared at the duck, but it made faces at me.

Motions: Place one finger at each side of your head. With the two fingers upright, move the remaining fingers of each hand up and down for "He wiggled his ears." Make hopping motions with tips of index and middle fingers on flat surface. Stop hopping while bunny stares. Wiggle nose for the last line.

The Lion Hunt

Let's go on a lion hunt. Okay? Are you afraid?
Say everything I say, and do everything I do, okay?
Here we go, I'm not afraid. (Children repeat.)

Tall grass! Have to go through it. Swish, swish, swish, swish.
(Brush sides of body with flat of hand.)
And down the road, I'm not afraid.

Big river! Have to swim it. Swim, swim, swim, swim.
(Continue descriptive motions here and below.)
And down the road, I'm not afraid.

Look at the mud, have to walk through it. Plop, plop, plop, plop.
And down the road, I'm not afraid.

Big mountain! Have to climb it. Climb, climb, climb, climb.
And down the other side, Roll, roll, roll, roll.
And down the road, I'm not afraid.

A dark cave. Let's explore it. Walk, walk, walk, walk.
What's that I feel?
Furry back! Long tail! Big fat tummy! Two big teeth!
It's a lion! Let's get out of here!

Big mountain! Have to climb it. Climb, climb, climb, climb.
And down the other side. Roll, roll, roll, roll.
And down the road, run, run, run, run.

Look at the mud, have to walk through it. Plop, plop, plop, plop.
And down the road, run, run, run, run.

Big river! Have to swim it. Swim, swim, swim, swim.
And down the road, run, run, run, run.

Tall grass! Have to go through it. Swish, swish, swish, swish.
And down the road, run, run, run, run.

There's my house.
Open the door, shut the door, up the stairs, in my room, under my bed.
Whew! I'm not afraid.

Assorted Finger Plays

Teacher starts the story:

"One morning when I was sitting looking out the window, I saw a cloud of
dust way off on the horizon, and as it got closer I could hear some singing
that sounded like this:"

The rest of the activity is by children:
Sing very softly:

We are the Beaver Patrol,
We are the Beaver Patrol,
We are the Beaver Patrol,
As marching along we go!

Count very softly and tap one finger on knee: 1, 2, 3, 4, 5, 6, 7, 8
Count softly and tap five fingers on knee: 1, 2, 3, 4, 5, 6, 7, 8
Count louder and slap knees with both hands: 1, 2, 3, 4, 5, 6, 7, 8
Count very loud and clap hands together: 1, 2, 3, 4, 5, 6, 7, 8
Sing boisterously:

We are the Beaver Patrol,
We are the Beaver Patrol,
We are the Beaver Patrol,
As marching along we go!   (*Continued*)

Repeat motions, reversing order: start with very loud and end with very soft voice. Whisper at the end—Good-bye!

Ten little cowboys feeling very fine,
One tripped on his spurs and then there were nine.
Nine little cowboys sat up very late,
One overslept and then there were eight.
Eight little cowboys riding off to heaven,
One stayed in Texas and then there were seven.
Seven little cowboys chopping up sticks,
One chopped himself in half and then there were six.
Six little cowboys very much alive,
One stole a rancher's cow, and then there were five.
Five little cowboys running through the door,
One couldn't turn the knob and then there were four.
Four little cowboys riding knee to knee,
One lost his stirrups and then there were three.
Three little cowboys wearing chaps quite new,
One found a rattlesnake and then there were two.
Two little cowboys resting in the sun,
One got all sunburned and then there was one.
One little cowboy hadn't any gun,
He galloped home to find it and then there was none.

I had a big rubber balloon
Almost as big as the moon.
It floated so prettily on the air
When suddenly POP! it wasn't there.

Motions: Make large circle with both arms above head. Move hands from left to right in sweeping motion. At the word "pop" clap hands together loudly.

Ten little peas in a pea pod press
One grew, two grew, and so did all the rest.
They grew and they grew and they grew and they grew
And one day the pea pod POPPED!

Motions: Hold closed hands together, hiding fingers. Let one index finger come, then the other, and then all fingers. Separate closed hands and spread arms farther and farther apart as peas grow. Lower voice on the last line and bring hands together at the word "popped."

There were five in the bed and the little one said,
Move over, move over.

And they all rolled over and one fell out.
There were four in the bed and the little one said,
Move over, move over.
And they all rolled over and one fell out.
There were three in the bed and the little one said,
Move over, move over.
And they all rolled over and one fell out.
There were two in the bed and the little one said,
Move over, move over.
And they all rolled over and one fell out.
There was one in the bed and the little one said,
I'm lonesome, I'm lonesome.
So they all got up, got into the bed.
We're happy, we're happy.

Motions: Show five fingers; wiggle little finger for smallest child. Use bent arm to motion for "move over." Open hand and rotate it for rolling motion.

Ten little soldiers standing in a row,
They all bowed down to the captain so.
They marched to the left, they marched to the right,
They stood up straight, ready to fight,
When along came a man with a great big gun.
My, you should have seen those soldiers run!

Two little hands go clap, clap, clap.
Two little feet go tap, tap, tap.
One little fist goes thump, thump, thump.
Two little feet go jump, jump, jump.
One little body goes round, round, round.
All boys and girls sit quietly down.

Five little soldiers standing in a row,
Three stood straight and two just so.
Along came the captain and what do you think?
Up jumped those soldiers as quick as a wink!

Motions: Thumb and index finger touching, other fingers straight.

I'm so happy, clap, clap, clap,
I'm so happy, tap, tap, tap,
I'm so happy I turn around,
I'm so happy that I fall down.

Oh, Jack in the box, so very still,
Will you come up and see me?
Yes, I will!

Motions: Hide face and curl up. Spring up and clap hands over head at "Yes, I will!"

Baby's shoes,
Sister's shoes,
Mother's shoes,
Father's shoes,
Giant's shoes.

Motions: Move hands farther and farther apart.

Finger Plays About Indians Long Ago

The Indians are creeping, SHHHHHHHHH,
The Indians are creeping, SHHHHHHHHH.
They don't make a sound when their feet touch the ground.
The Indians are creeping.

The Indian through the forest goes
Softly on his tippy-toes.
Hush, hush, hush.
Bow and arrow on his back,
Feather in his hair so black.
Step, step, step,
Hush, hush, hush.

This is how the great big Indian beats upon the drum:
Hi ho, hi ho, hum!

We are the Indians strong and brave,
In our feathers and war paint,
Pow wow, pow wow.
We're the men of the golden cow.
We are the red men, feathers-in-our-head men,
Down among the dead men,
Pow wow, pow wow.
When we come from hunting afar,
Greeted by our happy squaw,
Pow wow, pow wow.

We're the men of the golden cow.
We are the red men, feathers-in-our-head men,
Down among the dead men,
Pow wow, pow wow.
We don't fight with sticks or stones.
We use bows and arrows, not bricks or bones,
Pow wow, pow wow.
We're the men of the golden cow.
We are the red men, feathers-in-our-head men,
Down among the dead men,
Pow wow, pow wow.

There were five great big Indians,
They stood so straight and tall,
They tried to fit in a little canoe,
And one of them did fall.

There were four great big Indians,
They stood so straight and tall,
They tried to fit in a little canoe,
And one of them did fall.

(Continue on until:)

There was one great big Indian,
He stood so straight and tall,
And he did fit in the little canoe,
And out of it he did not fall.

Five little Indians standing in a row,
First one said, My eyes are brown.
The second said, I'm a hunter of great renown.
The third one said, My hair is black.
The fourth one said, I carry arrows on my back.
The fifth one said, My drum I beat.
And all the little Indians stamped their feet.

Halloween Finger Plays

One little, two little, three little witches
Fly over haystacks, fly over ditches,
Slide down the moon without any hitches.
Hi ho! Halloween's here.

Horned owl's hooting, it's time to go riding.
Deep in the shadows are black bats hiding,
With gay little goblins sliding, sliding.
Hi ho! Halloween's here.

Stand on your head with a lopsided wiggle,
Tickle your little black cats till they giggle,
Swish through the clouds with a higgledy-piggle.
Hi ho! Halloween's here.

Five little pumpkins sitting on a gate,
The first one said, It's getting late.
The second one said, There's witches in the air.
The third one said, I don't care.
The fourth one said, Let's run, run, run.
The fifth one said, It's Halloween fun.
When WOOOOOOOOO went the wind
And out went the light,
And away ran the jack-o'-lanterns
On a Halloween night.

Five little jack-o'-lanterns sitting on a gate,
The first one said, It's getting late.
The second one said, I hear a noise.
The third one said, It's only some boys.
The fourth one said, Let's run, run, run.
The fifth one said, It's Halloween fun.
WOOOOOOOO went the wind
And out went the light,
And away ran the jack-o'-lanterns
On a Halloween night.

Jack-o'-lantern, jack-o'-lantern,
Big and yellow.
Jack-o'lantern, jack-o'-lantern,
Funny fellow
Shining in the night,
With your candle light
Scaring all the witches
With your BOO! BOO! BOO!

Indoor Games
for Rainy Days

7-Up

Choose seven children to stand in a line at the front of the room. The remaining children sit in a U shape. Ask the seated children to close their eyes and keep them closed until you tell them to open them. The seven children quietly walk to the seated children and each touches one child softly on the head. As each child is touched, he or she raises one hand to ensure that he or she will only be touched once. When the seven children have touched one child each, they return to the front of the room and the seated children lower their hands.

Tell the children to open their eyes. Ask those whose heads were touched to raise their hands. These children get three guesses to try to name the person who touched them. If they are successful in naming the person, they exchange places with that person. If they do not guess who touched them, they remain seated. If you have fewer than fifteen children, you might play 5-Up, and give the children two guesses.

Dog and the Bone

The children sit in a U shape. One child (the dog) sits on a chair at the front of the group with an object (the bone) nearby on the floor. Blindfold this child and then point to a child to come up without being heard to get the bone. If the dog hears the child approaching, the dog can bark and point at the child. If the dog points directly at the approaching child, that child must be seated where he or she was caught. If the dog does not, and the child retrieves the bone and returns to the original place, then this second child becomes the dog.

Whose Voice?

The children are seated in a circle. One child is sent out of the room. Point to one child, who then hides from view. When the first child returns to the classroom, say, "Will the person who is hiding say Hello three times." (The children who hide should use their own voices. Later in the year, you can ask the children to disguise their voices.) The child gets three guesses to name the child who is hidden. The children can either identify the voice or see who is missing from the circle. This game cannot be played until the children have become acquainted with one another (perhaps two months after the start of school).

Hot Potato

The children stand or sit in a circle. Give a child an object which will be passed from hand to hand as the music plays. When the music stops, whoever is caught holding the object is out of the game and has to sit in the middle of the circle. The game continues until ten children are caught. A few rules have to be set up before starting this game:
1. No throwing of the object which is being passed. It must be passed from hand to hand.
2. No passing of the object after the music stops.

Who's the Leader?

The children sit or stand in a circle. One child is sent out of the room. Point to another child, who becomes the leader. This child leads the group by doing things with the hands, feet, or body, and the other children imitate all movements. (Actions might include stamping feet, clapping hands, snapping fingers, bending or swaying, or jumping.) When the child is brought back into the room, the leader has already started the motions. The important thing for the leader to remember is not to change the motion until the guessing child is looking at someone else. The child gets three guesses to name the leader.

Here Sits a Monkey

(See Chapter VI, Music, for directions.)

Huckle, Buckle, Beanstalk

After being shown an object, all the children but one are asked to leave the room. (Set up rules for hall behaviors before the game.) The child who remains hides the object, but it must remain partially visible. When the children return to the room, they search for the object. If they find it, they do not say anything nor point to it. They walk off to another part of the room (so as not to give away the hiding place) and then to a designated spot where they say, "Huckle, Buckle, Beanstalk." After most of the children have located the object, help those who are left by calling "warm" or "hot" if they get near the object, and "cold" or "cool" if they are far from it.

The idea of this game is to pretend that you didn't see it, so that you won't give away the hiding place.

Stir the Soup

The children sit in chairs in a large circle. One child is designated the cook. The cook chooses children as ingredients for the soup and names them as they are picked to join in the soup (onion, carrots, meat, salt, pepper, potatoes). When five or six children have been chosen, the cook announces that the soup is almost ready and that it needs to be stirred three times. The child holds a ladle or rhythm stick. The cook hits the floor with the stick three times. The cook and all the ingredients run for the empty seats. Whoever is left standing becomes the new cook. (Note: Use one fewer chairs than children.)

Musical Chairs

(See Chapter VI, Music, for directions.)

Cut the Cherry Pie

The children stand in a circle with hands joined (ask them not to squeeze their partner's hand). One child skips around the outside of the circle as the children chant:

I cut the cherry pie,

I cut the cherry pie,

Cut, cut, cut, cut.

I cut the cherry pie, and get out of the way.

To cut the cherry pie, the child on the outside of the circle strikes a pair of joined hands with the edge of his or her hand and steps back out of the way. The children whose hands were touched drop hands and each run in opposite directions around the circle. The first one back to the original place becomes the cutter.

Mousetrap #1

The children stand in a circle one behind the other. When the music starts, they march through a bridge formed by two children holding their arms high. When the music stops the children of the bridge bring their arms down and try to trap someone inside. The first child caught sits inside the circle. When a second child is caught, he or she forms a bridge with the first child who was caught. They take their place at another part of the circle. The game continues until five traps are made. Then it begins all over again.

Mousetrap #2

The children stand in a circle facing inward. They join hands (ask them not to squeeze their neighbor's hand). Four children are designated the mice.

When the music plays, the mice run in and out of the trap. When the music stops, the children bring their hands down quickly to trap the mice inside. Any children caught become part of the trap. You might choose to replace the children as they are caught.

Squirrels in the Tree

Since this game can become rather complicated, and in order to be fair to all the children, you will need to mark down on paper which children will be squirrels and which trees. As the children and you become more familiar with the game, making notes will not be necessary.

The children are divided into sets of three. Two children form the tree and the third child is the squirrel. Spread the trees around the room. If you have twenty-five children, you will need eight trees. One child (squirrel) will be left without a tree. When the music plays, the squirrels leave their trees and play at some distance from them. When the music stops, the squirrels seek shelter in the trees (one squirrel to a tree). The child who does not find a tree is *not* out of the game. Play the game three times without having children change their positions. If you think the children can remember, you can name them ones, twos, or threes; in the first set the ones and twos are trees; in the second set, the twos and threes are trees; and in the last set, the threes and ones are trees.

Poison Pond

Two different areas will have to be designated in the room—one a safe place and the other a poison pond (a carpet can serve as the pond). When the music starts the children run in and out of the pond. When the music stops, any child found in the pond is "dead" and is out of the game.

Transitional Activities

1. *Finger Plays.* (See the first section in the Appendix.)
2. *I Spy.* Use colors in the beginning of the year; use numbers or members in a set after these mathematical concepts have been introduced. At first, *you* start the game; when the children understand the game, let them take over. Let the leader whisper the answer in your ear before the others begin to guess.
3. Describe an object with words. The children may use a given number of questions to name the object.
4. Have a collection of objects in a very large paper sack. Let the children, one at a time, reach their hands in and tell what the object is that is in their hands. If a child cannot name the object, ask for a description of how it feels.
5. In a large paper sack hide a number of objects that make sounds. As each sound is made, the children try to guess something about the objects making the sounds or try to name the objects.
6. Give the children a series of directions to follow. They may not begin following the instructions until you have finished giving the total instruction. For example:

   Stand up, turn around two times, and sit down.
   Stand up, jump into the air, turn around, and sit down.

   Start with three simple directions and later add one or two additional directions.
7. Talk about the meaning of the word *opposite* and give the children an example or two. Then start the game. Give the children a word and then ask for a word meaning the opposite of it.
8. Take one of the children's names and see how many words they can think of that sound the very same at the beginning. Practice the sound first. Start with a consonant; *S* is a good letter to start with.
9. Describe the clothing of one of the children and see if the children can guess who it is. Limit the number of guesses.

10. Work on prepositions such as *over, under, beside, in, inside, behind, near.* Use a large cardboard box to let the children demonstrate the meaning of each word.

11. Show an item new to the room which the children would find interesting. Let them tell you things about it. Keep track of how many things they can tell you about it.

12. Read some nursery rhymes and talk about how the words at the end of the lines sound alike:

Hickory, dickory *dock.*

The mouse ran up the *clock.*

Give the children some examples of pairs of rhyming words: *boy, toy; silk, milk; land, sand.* Then give them one word and ask them to give you some words that rhyme with it.

13. Give the children the names of objects belonging to a particular classification. Ask the children if they can name that classification. Examples: ring, necklace, and bracelet belong to the set of jewelry; boat, car, airplane, and truck belong to the set of transportation vehicles or things that can move.

14. Hide something in a box and tell the children three or four things about it. See if they can name the object.

15. *Charades.* Let each child act out a word that involves movement such as washing, brushing, sweeping, sawing, hammering, ironing, writing, or singing. The rest of the class tries to name the action.

16. Read a couple of nonsense poems; or read several poems about animals; or read several poems about transportation vehicles.

17. Show the children a number of fingers. Ask them if they have another way to show that many fingers. Examples: Show two fingers on one hand; the child responds by showing one finger on each hand. Show five fingers of one hand; the child responds by showing two fingers on one hand and three on the other.

18. Start a game by saying, "I'm going to San Antonio." The first child repeats the same and then says, "I'm taking. . . ." and adds another word starting with the same letter as the *place* in the first statement. Example: "I'm going to *San* Antonio and I'm taking my *suitcase.*" The second child might say, "I'm going to *San* Antonio and I'm taking my *suitcase* and my *silly* putty."

19. Ask the children how they could help you know what something looked like if you did not know what the word meant. Examples: dog, giraffe, car.

20. Start to tell a story that is either very funny or very exciting. Stop and let a child go on with what he or she thinks happened next. Pick up from this statement, add another sentence or so, and then let another child go on with the story. After a number of children have added their ideas, find a way to end the story.

21. Find an odd picture. Some photographs are made by using trick photography to produce very strange subject matter. Show this to the children for their comments.

22. Sing a song that requires the children to make up words to fill in certain lines. Ask what Johnny should do in the song "Johnny Get Your Hair Cut" from *American Folk Songs for Children*; or substitute a child's name in the song and tell him or her what to do. Example: "Mary, brush your teeth, teeth, teeth." In the song "Aiken Drum" from *Treasury of Folk Songs,* the children can sing about the clothing, Example:

His coat was made of chocolate bits.

His hair was made of shredded wheat.

23. Tell a simple story which includes information about numbers of animals. Example: "I was walking on the street one day, and I met one tyrannosaur and two brontosaurs. How many dinosaurs did I see?"

24. Tell a tall tale and let the children tell one also.

25. Have a number of small objects in your hand (not more than five). Show them to the children and then hide them. Ask how many items were in your hand and what they were.

26. Show the children one object or picture. After letting them observe it for a minute or so, hide it from them and see how many things they can tell you about it.

27. Ask the children if they know words that sound alike but have different meanings. If you get no response, print the following pairs of words on the chalkboard and talk about the differences:

male	mail
tail	tale
fare	fair
can	can
knight	night

28. Let the children make a sad face, a funny face, a mad face, or a happy face.

29. Say:

Touch your ears, *or* Put your fingers on your ears.

Touch your cheeks, *or* Put your fingers on your cheeks.

Touch your _____.

Name various body parts. Touch the same places on yourself. To catch the children, touch a part different than what you name. Example: Say, "Touch your knees," and put your fingers on your head.

30. Say:

Roll them, roll them, roll them,

Faster, faster, faster,

　Touch your chest.

(Children roll one hand over the other as they hold them in front of their chests.)

Roll them, roll them, roll them,
Faster, faster, faster,
 Touch your _____.

Name various body parts. To end the game, insert in place of "faster"—
"Slower, slower, slower; please sit still!"

Good Books
for Children

Andersen, Hans Christian. *The Emperor's New Clothes*. Illustrated by Virginia Lee Burton. Houghton Mifflin, 1949.

Anderson, Clarence William. *Billy and Blaze*. Macmillan, 1936.

―――――. *Blaze and the Forest Fire*. Macmillan, 1948.

―――――. *Blaze and Thunderbolt*. Macmillan, 1955.

―――――. *Blaze and the Mountain Lion*. Macmillan, 1959.

Anglund, Joan Walsh. *In a Pumpkin Shell: A Mother Goose ABC*. Harcourt Brace Jovanovich, 1960.

Ardizzone, Edward. *Little Tim and the Brave Sea Captain*. Oxford University Press, 1955.

Asbjornsen, Peter Christen. *The Three Billy Goats Gruff*. Illustrated by Marcia Brown. Harcourt Brace Jovanovich, 1957.

―――――. *The Three Billy Goats Gruff*. Illustrated by Susan Blair. Scholastic Book Services, 1963.

Barrett, Judith. *Animals Should Definitely Not Wear Clothing*. Atheneum, 1970.

Bemelmans, Ludwig. *Madeline*. Viking, 1939.

―――――. *Madeline's Rescue*. Viking, 1953.

―――――. *Madeline in London*. Viking, 1961.

Berwick, Jean. *Arthur and the Golden Guinea*. Golden Gate Junior Books, 1963.

Beskow, Elsa. *Pelle's New Suit*. Harper & Row, 1929.

Bishop, Claire. *The Five Chinese Brothers*. Coward, McCann & Geoghegan, 1938.

Bridwell, Norman. *Clifford, the Big Red Dog*. Scholastic Book Services, 1969.

―――――. *Clifford Takes a Trip*. Scholastic Book Services, 1969, 1973.

Bright, Robert. *Georgie*. Doubleday, 1944.

―――――. *Georgie and the Robbers*. Doubleday, 1963.

Brown, Marcia. *Stone Soup*. Scribner's, 1947.

_____. *Dick Wittingham and His Cat*. Scribner's, 1950.

_____. *Puss in Boots*. Scribner's, 1952.

Brown, Margaret Wise. *The Noisy Book*. Harper & Row, 1939.

_____. *The Country Noisy Book*. Harper & Row, 1940.

_____. *Wait Till the Moon Is Full*. Harper & Row, 1948.

_____. *The Quiet Noisy Book*. Harper & Row, 1950.

_____. *The Golden Bunny*. Golden Press, 1953.

Bryant, Sara Cone. *Epaminondas and His Auntie*. Houghton Mifflin, 1938.

_____. *The Burning Rice Fields*. Holt, Rinehart and Winston, 1963.

Bulla, Clyde Robert. *Poppy Seeds*. Crowell, 1955.

Burningham, John. *Mr. Gumpy's Outing*. Holt, Rinehart and Winston, 1970.

Burton, Virginia Lee. *Choo Choo*. Houghton Mifflin, 1937.

_____. *Mike Mulligan and His Steam Shovel*. Houghton Mifflin, 1939.

_____. *The Little House*. Houghton Mifflin, 1942.

_____. *Katy and the Big Snow*. Houghton Mifflin, 1943.

Carle, Eric. *The Very Hungry Caterpillar*. World, 1970.

_____. *Do You Want to Be My Friend?* Thomas Y. Crowell, 1971.

_____. *My Very First Book of Colors*. Thomas Y. Crowell, 1974.

Chandler, Edna Walker. *Five Cent, Five Cent*. Whitman, 1967.

Charlip, Remy. *Fortunately*. Parents' Magazine Press, 1964.

_____. *Mother, Mother, I Feel Sick*. Parents' Magazine Press, 1966.

Clark, Margery. *Three Stories from the Poppy Seed Cakes*. Scholastic Book Services, 1972.

Coombs, Patricia. *Dorrie and the Blue Witch*. Lothrop, Lee & Shepard, 1964.

Daugherty, James Henry. *Andy and the Lion*. Viking, 1938.

De Angeli, Marguerite Lofft. *Book of Nursery Rhymes and Mother Goose Rhymes*. Doubleday, 1954.

Dennis, Wesley. *Flip*. Viking, 1941.

De Regniers, Beatrice Schenk. *What Can You Do With a Shoe?* Harper & Row, 1955.

_____. *May I Bring a Friend?* Atheneum, 1964.

_____. *Willy O'Dwyer Jumped in the Fire*. Atheneum, 1968.

Du Bois, William Pene. *Otto in Texas*. Viking, 1959.

Duvoisin, Roger Antoine. *Petunia*. Knopf, 1950.

_____. *Petunia's Christmas*. Knopf, 1952.

_____. *Veronica*. Knopf, 1961.

Eichenberg, Fritz. *Ape in a Cape*. Harcourt Brace Jovanovich, 1952.

_____. *Dancing in the Moon*. Harcourt Brace Jovanovich, 1955.

Emberley, Barbara. *Drummer Hoff.* Prentice-Hall, 1967.

Emberley, Ed. *The Wing on a Flea.* Little, Brown, 1961.

Ets, Marie Hall. *In the Forest.* Viking, 1944.

————. *Play with Me.* Viking, 1955.

————. *Gilberto and the Wind.* Viking, 1963.

————. *Just Me.* Viking, 1965.

Evans, Katherine. *The Man, the Boy and the Donkey.* Albert Whitman, 1958.

Fatio, Louise. *The Happy Lion.* Whittlesey, 1954.

Flack, Marjorie. *Angus and the Ducks.* Doubleday, 1930.

————. *Angus and the Cat.* Doubleday, 1931.

————. *Ask Mr. Bear.* Macmillan, 1932.

————. *The Story About Ping.* Viking, 1933.

————. *Wait for William.* Houghton Mifflin, 1935.

Freeman, Don. *Mop Top.* Viking, 1955.

————. *Norman the Doorman.* Viking, 1959.

————. *The Turtle and the Dove.* Viking, 1964.

————. *Corduroy.* Viking, 1968.

Friskey, Margaret. *Johnny and the Monarch.* Childrens, 1946.

————. *Indian Two Feet and His Horse.* Childrens, 1959.

————. *The Seven Diving Ducks.* Childrens, 1965.

————. *Indian Two Feet and His Eagle Feather.* Childrens, 1967.

Gag, Wanda. *Millions of Cats.* Coward, McCann & Geoghegan, 1928.

————. *ABC Bunny.* Coward, McCann & Geoghegan, 1933.

Galdone, Paul. *Old Mother Hubbard and Her Dog.* McGraw-Hill, 1960.

Gantos, Jack. *Rotten Ralph.* Houghton Mifflin, 1976.

Gramatky, Hardie. *Little Toot.* Putnam, 1939.

————. *Little Toot on the Thames.* Putnam, 1964.

Greenaway, Kate. *A Apple Pie.* Warne, 1917.

Grimm, Jakob. *Snow White and Rose Red.* Scribner's, 1964.

————. *Rumpelstilskin.* Harcourt Brace Jovanovich, 1967.

————. *The Magic Fish.* Scholastic Book Services, 1967.

————. *The Bremen Town Musicians.* McGraw-Hill, 1968.

————. *The Fisherman and His Wife.* Follett, 1969.

————. *Clever Kate.* Macmillan, 1973.

Guilfoile, Elizabeth. *Nobody Listens to Andrew.* Follett, 1957.

Hader, Berta and Elmer. *The Big Snow.* Macmillan, 1948.

Handforth, Thomas. *Mei Li.* Doubleday, 1938.

Harris, Joel Chandler. *The Favorite Uncle Remus.* Houghton Mifflin, 1948.

Hillert, Margaret. *The Three Bears.* Follett, 1963.

Hoban, Russell. *Bedtime for Frances.* Harper & Row, 1960.

———. *Bread and Jam for Frances.* Harper & Row, 1964.

———. *A Baby Sister for Frances.* Harper & Row, 1964.

———. *A Bargain for Frances.* Harper & Row, 1970.

Hoff, Sydney. *Danny and the Dinosaur.* Harper & Row, 1958.

———. *Julius.* Harper & Row, 1959.

———. *Where's Prancer?* Harper & Row, 1960.

Hogan, Inez. *The Littlest Bear.* Dutton, 1959.

Holl, Adelaide. *Rain Puddle.* Lothrop, Lee & Shepard, 1965.

———. *The Runaway Giant.* Lothrop, Lee & Shepard, 1967.

———. *The ABC of Cars, Trucks and Machines.* McGraw-Hill, 1970.

Ipcar, Dahlov. *The Wonderful Egg.* Doubleday, 1958.

Jacobs, Leland Blaire. *Just around the Corner.* Holt, Rinehart and Winston, 1964.

Janosch. *Dear Snowman.* World, 1970.

Johnson, Crockett. *Harold and the Purple Crayon.* Harper & Row, 1955.

Joslin, Sesyle. *What Do You Do, Dear?* Young Scott Books, 1961.

Kahl, Virginia. *Away Went Wolfgang.* Scribner's, 1954.

———. *The Duchess Bakes a Cake.* Scribner's, 1955.

———. *Plum Pudding for Christmas.* Scribner's, 1956.

Keats, Ezra Jack. *The Snowy Day.* Viking, 1962.

———. *Whistle for Willie.* Viking, 1964.

———. *Jennie's Hat.* Harper & Row, 1966.

———. *Peter's Chair.* Harper & Row, 1967.

———. *A Letter for Amy.* Harper & Row, 1968.

———. *Goggles.* Macmillan, 1969.

———. *Pet Show.* Macmillan, 1972.

Kepes, Juliet. *Ladybird, Quickly.* Little, Brown, 1964.

Konkle, Janet. *J. Hamilton Hamster.* Childrens, 1957.

Krasilovsky, Phyllis. *The Man Who Didn't Wash His Dishes.* Doubleday, 1950.

———. *The Cow Who Fell in the Canal.* Doubleday, 1957.

Kraus, Robert. *Leo, the Late Bloomer.* Windmill Books, Dutton, 1973.

———. *The Littlest Rabbit.* Scholastic Book Services, 1973.

Krauss, Ruth. *The Carrot Seed.* Harper & Row, 1945.

———. *The Growing Story.* Harper & Row, 1947.

———. *A Hole Is to Dig.* Harper & Row, 1952.

———. *A Very Special House.* Harper & Row, 1953.

La Fontaine. *The Lion and the Rat.* Illustrated by Brian Wildsmith. Franklin Watts, 1963.

————. *The North Wind and the Sun.* Illustrated by Brian Wildsmith. Franklin Watts, 1964.

————. *The Rich Man and the Shoemaker.* Illustrated by Brian Wildsmith. Franklin Watts, 1965.

————. *The Hare and the Tortoise.* Illustrated by Brian Wildsmith. Franklin Watts, 1966.

Langstaff, John M. *Frog Went A-'Courtin.* Harcourt Brace Jovanovich, 1955.

————. *Over in the Meadow.* Harcourt Brace Jovanovich, 1957.

Leaf, Munro. *The Story of Ferdinand.* Viking, 1936.

————. *Noodle.* Scholastic Book Services, 1969.

Lenski, Lois. *Cowboy Small.* Oxford University Press, 1949.

Lindgren, Astrid. *Tomtem.* Coward, McCann & Geoghegan, 1961.

————. *Tomtem and the Fox.* Coward, McCann & Geoghegan, 1966.

Lionni, Leo. *Little Blue and Little Yellow.* Ivan Obolensky, 1959.

————. *Inch by Inch.* Ivan Obolensky, 1960.

————. *Swimmy.* Pantheon, 1963.

————. *Tico and the Golden Wings.* Pantheon, 1964.

————. *Frederick.* Pantheon, 1967.

————. *The Biggest House in the World.* Pantheon, 1968.

————. *Alexander and the Wind-Up Mouse.* Pantheon, 1969.

————. *Fish Is Fish.* Pantheon, 1970.

Lipkind, William, and Nicolas Mordrinoff. *Finders Keepers.* Harcourt Brace Jovanovich, 1951.

Lobel, Arnold. *Prince Bertram the Bad.* Harper & Row, 1963.

————. *Frog and Toad Are Friends.* Harper & Row, 1970.

————. *Frog and Toad Together.* Harper & Row, 1972.

Lund, Doris. *Attic of the Wind.* Parents' Magazine Press, 1966.

Martin, William Ivan. *Brown Bear, Brown Bear, What Do You See?* Holt, Rinehart and Winston, 1970.

Mayer, Mercer. *There's a Nightmare in My Closet.* Dial, 1968.

————. *Just for You.* Golden Press, 1975.

McCloskey, Robert. *Lentil.* Viking, 1940.

————. *Make Way for Ducklings.* Viking, 1941.

————. *Blueberries for Sal.* Viking, 1948.

————. *One Morning in Maine.* Viking, 1952.

————. *Burt-Dow Deep Water Man.* Viking, 1963.

McGinley, Phyllis. *All Around the Town.* Lippincott, 1948.

Mendoza, George. *The Marcel Marceau Counting Book.* Doubleday, 1971.

Miles, Miska. *The Rabbit Garden*. Little, Brown, 1967.

Milhous, Katherine. *The Egg Tree*. Scribner's, 1950.

Minarik, Else Homelund. *Little Bear*. Harper & Row, 1957.

_____ . *Little Bear's Visit*. Harper & Row, 1961.

_____ . *A Kiss for Little Bear*. Harper & Row, 1968.

Moore, Clement. *The Night Before Christmas*. Grosset & Dunlap, 1949.

Moore, Eva. *Johnny Appleseed*. Scholastic Book Services, 1970.

Moore, Lilian. *Little Raccoon and the Thing in the Pool*. Whittlesey, 1953.

Mosel, Arlene. *Tikki, Tikki, Tembo*. Scholastic Book Services, 1974.

Munari, Bruno. *Bruno Munari's ABC*. Wm. Collins & World, 1960.

Nodset, Joan L. *Go Away Dog*. Harper & Row, 1963.

_____ . *Who Took the Farmer's Hat?* Harper & Row, 1963.

Payne, Emmy. *Katy No Pocket*. Houghton Mifflin, 1944.

Polito, Leo. *Little Leo*. Scribner's, 1951.

Potter, Beatrix. *The Tale of Peter Rabbit*. Frederick Warne, 1903.

Quigley, Lillian. *The Blind Men and the Elephant*. Scribner's, 1959.

Rey, H. A. *Curious George*. Houghton Mifflin, 1941.

_____ . *Curious George Takes a Job*. Houghton Mifflin, 1947.

Rey, Margaret. *Pretzel*. Harper & Row, 1944.

Rojankovsky, Feodor. *The Tall Book of Mother Goose*. Harper & Row, 1942.

Scheer, Julian. *Rain Makes Applesauce*. Holiday House, 1964.

Sendak, Maurice. *Where the Wild Things Are*. Harper & Row, 1963.

_____ . *In the Night Kitchen*. Harper & Row, 1970.

Shaw, Charles G. *It Looked Like Spilt Milk*. Harper & Row, 1947.

Sherlock, Philip M. *Anansi the Spider Man*. Thomas Y. Crowell, 1954.

Slobodkina, Esphyr. *Caps for Sale*. Scholastic Book Services, 1940.

Spilka, Arnold. *Paint All Kinds of Pictures*. Henry Z. Walck, 1963.

Steptoe, John. *Stevie*. Harper & Row, 1969.

Swift, Hildegarde H. *The Little Red Lighthouse and the Great Gray Bridge*. Harcourt Brace Jovanovich, 1942.

Tresselt, Alvin. *The Rabbit Story*. Lothrop, Lee & Shepard, 1957.

_____ . *The Frog in the Well*. Lothrop, Lee & Shepard, 1958.

_____ . *The Mitten: An Old Ukrainian Tale*. Lothrop, Lee & Shepard, 1964.

Tworkov, Jack. *The Camel Who Took a Walk*. Aladdin, 1951.

Udry, Janice May. *A Tree Is Nice*. Harper & Row, 1956.

_____ . *Let's Be Enemies*. Harper & Row, 1961.

_____ . *What Mary Jo Shared*. Whitman, 1966.

Ungerer, Tomi. *One, Two, Where's My Shoe?* Harper & Row, 1964.

Waber, Bernard. *Ira Sleeps Over*. Houghton Mifflin, 1972.

Ward, Lynd. *The Biggest Bear.* Houghton Mifflin, 1952.

Weil, Lisl. *The Sorcerer's Apprentice.* Little, Brown, 1962.

Weise, Kurt. *Fish in the Air.* Viking, 1948.

Wildsmith, Brian. *Brian Wildsmith's ABC.* Franklin Watts, 1962.

————. *Brian Wildsmith's Mother Goose.* Franklin Watts, 1964.

————. *Brian Wildsmith's 1, 2, 3's.* Franklin Watts, 1965.

————. *Brian Wildsmith's Wild Animals.* Franklin Watts, 1967.

————. *Brian Wildsmith's Birds.* Franklin Watts, 1967.

————. *Brian Wildsmith's Fishes.* Franklin Watts, 1968.

————. *Squirrels.* Franklin Watts, 1975.

Yashima, Taro. *Crow Boy.* Viking, 1955.

————. *Umbrella.* Viking, 1958.

Ylla. *Two Little Bears.* Harper & Row, 1954.

Zaffo, George J. *The Big Book of Real Trains.* Grosset & Dunlap, 1949.

————. *The Big Book of Real Trucks.* Grosset & Dunlap, 1950.

————. *Airplanes and Trucks and Trains, Fire Engines, Boats and Ships and Building and Wrecking Machines.* Grosset & Dunlap, 1968

————. *The Big Book of Real Boats and Ships.* Grosset & Dunlap, 1972.

Zion, Gene. *Harry the Dirty Dog.* Harper & Row, 1956.

————. *No Roses for Harry.* Harper & Row, 1958.

————. *Harry by the Sea.* Harper & Row, 1965.

Zolotow, Charlotte. *The Storm Book.* Harper & Row, 1952.

————. *A Tiger Named Thomas.* Lothrop, Lee & Shepard, 1963.

————. *The Hating Book.* Harper & Row, 1969.

Kindergarten Supply Sources

Childcraft Education Corporation
20 Kilmer Road
Edison, NJ 08817
or
964 3rd Avenue
New York, NY 10022

Cole Supply
P.O. Box 1717
(103 E. Bird)
Pasadena, TX 77502

Creative Publications
P.O. Box 10328
Palo Alto, CA 94303

Heffernan School Supply Co., Inc.
P.O. Box 5309
(2111 West Avenue)
San Antonio, TX 78201

Jericho, Inc.
P.O. Box 6591
Houston, TX 77005

Practical Drawing Company
P.O. Box 5388
(2205 Cockrell and 12215 Coit Road)
Dallas, TX 75222

Spéco Educational Systems
3210 Belt Line Road, Suite 140
Dallas, TX 75234

Kindergarten
Media Resources

Let's Find Out and *See Saw News*
Scholastic Book Services
902 Sylvan Avenue
Englewood Cliffs, NJ 07632

National Geographic World
National Geographic Society
Department 01075
17th and M Street NW
Washington, DC 20036

Ranger Rick Nature Magazine
National Wildlife Federation
1412 16th Street NW
Washington, DC 20036

Weekly Reader Surprise
Xerox Publications
Education Center
Columbus, OH 43216

Fearon Teacher-Aid Books...
The Idea Books That Free You to Teach

More related titles from Fearon Pitman's high-motivation Teacher-Aid line include:

COOL COOKING FOR KIDS: Recipes and Nutrition for Preschoolers; P. McClenahan and I. Jaqua. A comprehensive "idea" book on nutrition and cooking techniques for teachers of very small children. Management suggestions, recipes, resources on nutrition, health notes. 9" × 6"; 176 pages; line art.   #1614-X

THE EARLY CHILDHOOD ACTIVITY SERIES; Sara Throop. Key questions and discussions about basic concepts in science (animal and plant life, weather, motion, etc.); in health and safety; in mathematics (making comparisons, counting, time, and other basics); in social studies (a child's-eye view of anthropology, sociology, etc.); and in language arts (vocabulary, expression, etc.).   All 5-1/2" × 8-1/4"; illus.

Science for the Young Child; 72 pages.   #6302-4

Health and Safety for the Young Child; 72 pages.   #5410-6

Mathematics for the Young Child; 72 pages.   #4425-9

Social Studies for the Young Child; 72 pages.   #6425-X

Language Arts for the Young Child; 72 pages.   #4205-1

NURSERY SCHOOL AND DAY CARE CENTER MANAGEMENT GUIDE, Revised Edition; Clare Cherry, Barbara Harkness, and Kay Kuzma. Completely revised, this total plan and systematic guide for establishing and running a nursery school, kindergarten, and full day care center is a must for your daily reference.   8-1/2" × 11"; 352 pages; 3-ring binder.   #4791-6

150 PLUS! GAMES AND ACTIVITIES FOR EARLY CHILDHOOD; Zane Spencer. For any teacher of preschool children; here are over 150 activities for readiness skills, motor skills, and more. All activities are easy to set up and manage.   6" × 9"; 160 pages; illus.   #5068-2

PRESCHOOL GAMES AND ACTIVITIES; Sandra Taetzsch and Lyn Taetzsch. Help children develop skills for success in school, via physical activities, number and letter games, crafts. Over 100 games and activities, with even more variations.   6" × 9"; 108 pages; illus.   #5605-2

FREE AND INEXPENSIVE MATERIALS FOR PRESCHOOL AND EARLY CHILDHOOD, Second Edition; Robert Monahan. Over 400 items for early-childhood or primary-grade teacher to obtain free or at little cost. Films, books, pamphlets, posters.   5-1/2" × 8-1/2"; 126 pages.   #3175-0

For a complete Teacher-Aid catalog, write **Fearon Pitman Publishers, Inc.,** 6 Davis Drive, Belmont, California 94002. Or telephone (415) 592-7810.